MW00635137

Back to School, Back to Life

Back to School, Back to Life

Helping Children and Adolescents Return from the COVID-19 Pandemic

Beth Lusby, Ph.D.
Sheryl R. Jackson, Ph.D.

Printed in the United States of America

The material in this book is intended for information and education and does not substitute for individual diagnosis, assessment, or treatment by a qualified medical professional or therapist. No expressed or implied guarantee as to the benefit of the included information can be given nor liability taken.

Library of Congress Cataloging-in-Publication Data

Lusby, Beth Jackson, Sheryl

Back to school, back to life : Helping children and adolescents return from the COVID-19 pandemic/ Beth Lusby, Ph.D. Sheryl R. Jackson, Ph.D.

ISBN-13: 978-1-7373224-0-5

Cover and Interior Illustrations by Conor Cole

To my amazing colleague, Sheri, for helping me finally follow through on writing a book. To Ron, Sydney, and Maddi for general support and cheerleading. To the families who trust me to work alongside them to find progress and growth.

—— BL

To Beth for her friendship and unending collegial support. To Caden, Conor, and Rainey for offering love and encouragement. To the courageous clients who have shared their journey with me. To the courageous families and children that are diligently working to rise from the pandemic year stronger and more purposeful than before.

—— SRJ

DISCLAIMER

Every child and every family is unique. The information provided in this book is not meant to replace assessment, diagnosis, or treatment by trained professionals.

This book offers general information that is likely to be relevant to many but is not individualized for each family and each child.

We encourage you to consider seeking professional help if your situation is more serious or exceeds the scope of the helpful suggestions from this book.

ACKNOWLEDGEMENTS

There are so many wonderful people to thank for their contribution and support throughout the writing process. Special thanks go to Susan Efseaff for her read through and helpful ideas. We are incredibly thankful to Conor Cole for his working and re-working illustrations that were both cute and engaging. Much appreciation goes to Gillian Humphrey for her help with cover design. Additional thanks go to Steve and Shirley Humphrey, Ken Keene, Kathy Bell, Paul Keene, and Morgan Sanchez for their support and ever-listening ears. Our children were a great source of inspiration and support as well: Caden, Sydney, Maddi, Conor, and Rainey.

CONTENTS

OTHER CONCERNS FOR RETURN TO SCHOOL

GENERAL CONCERNS FOR RETURN TO LIFE

ADDITIONAL READING

INTRODUCTION

"You gain strength, courage, and confidence by every experience in which you really stop to look fear in the face. You are able to say to yourself, 'I have lived through this horror. I can take the next thing that comes along.' You must do the thing you think you cannot do".

— ELEANOR ROOSEVELT

CHAPTER 1

Why This Book

The pandemic has presented special concerns and challenges to parents as they try to balance safety, education, social development, and family peace under unprecedented circumstances. Individual decisions regarding when and how to return children to school are highly personal and complex. The aim of this book is to address some of these concerns, provide comfort, and offer guidance.

As psychologists working in suburban America, we have had an interesting window into some of the experiences and struggles of families as they strive to respond effectively to the pandemic. During the past year, we have developed ideas and strategies, based on sound psychological practices, knowledge of psychological research, and clinical experience, to help families navigate a variety of pandemic related challenges.

A concern of many parents has been when and how to return children to in-person school. In some areas of the country, schools have reopened and are offering a variety of options for parents to consider. They are allowing families to choose whether students attend in-person or virtual classrooms, or some combination of these options. In other areas of the country, schools are not yet available for in-person instruction. By the fall of 2021, most schools will be back in person. Some schools will offer options while others will not.

This book is not directed toward every family. Families that are satisfied with online education and are staying with that mode will have limited need for our suggestions. Families that are in financial distress, requiring children to return to school regardless of their ideal preference, may benefit from some of the suggestions to reduce anxiety. There are also many families for whom the return to in-person education will be easy, celebrated, and loved without any anxiety, fears, or opposition. This book is simply not likely to be needed by those families.

Through this book, our aim is to help families consider a variety of factors regarding the return to school and offer thoughts on how to accomplish this goal successfully.

We make several underlying assumptions.

It is our belief that for most kids, returning to in-person school is important. There are several factors that contribute to our position. Education itself is vital (even though there is disagreement about what to teach and how things should be taught). Although some children and adolescents have found success through online or at-home education, the overwhelming majority are best served with at least some portion of in-person schooling. Ideally, in-person education allows for teachers to facilitate the education process based upon training and experience.

On average, current belief from parents, children, and teachers is that virtual education is less educational than its in-person counterpart. In-person school allows for a more multi-sensory educational experience. Hands-on learning such as that facilitated through labs, experiments, game play, and projects is more readily achieved when students are in the same room with teachers and peers.

For many youth, it may be several years in the future before we fully understand the true consequences of the shutdown on children. It's possible that everyone will be behind; it is also possible that the accelerated group suffers little while those who struggle will struggle more, creating a larger divide. In fact, the "Matthew Effect" in education refers to how the "rich get richer and the poor get poorer." For instance, good readers read more and become better readers, while struggling readers read less and fall further behind. Time will tell.

In addition to our belief in the academic benefits of in-person education, we also think social benefits are incredibly important. We learn to be social by being social. Socializing with others provides important feedback. When we pick our nose in public and others look at us with disgust, we learn to pick our nose in private. When we pick our nose in the privacy of our car at a stop light and turn to see the disgust on the face of a driver of another car, we learn that our car is not necessarily private (check out Seinfeld, Season 4, Episode 13).

In other words, sometimes feedback helps us understand what *not* to do as well as what *to* do. When the feedback is negative or uncomfortable, it is incredibly important that children learn how to manage it. Sometimes you alter your behavior (don't call Sally a bad name, others disapprove of bad language) and sometimes you ignore it (Jenny thinks my shoes are ugly but I love them, so I will ignore Jenny).

When the socialization occurring at school is reinforced by parental involvement, it can foster maturation and the deepening of values. Parents are integral in helping children know when to alter behavior and when to ignore feedback. When children are interacting online more than they are in-person, this feedback system can become confusing. Social media, in particular, offers feedback (you must be beautiful and successful by sixteen or you are a loser) and the medium makes it very difficult to evaluate the feedback appropriately (say, to understand that virtually no one is at the height of beauty or success at sixteen - as that's ridiculous!)

In addition to fostering academic and social positives, returning to in-person school also decreases some negative habits that may have increased during the pandemic. The reality is that many children who are attending virtual classes or online school are spending a great deal of time on electronic devices and social media. Some have become withdrawn from family members and close themselves off in their rooms. This isolation has several potential results: social skills become rusty, anxieties can become more pronounced, and struggles for independence, normal in adolescence, are interrupted. In addition, emotional and psychological growth can be stunted and educational development can be slowed (or halted).

Another negative that will hopefully decrease with the return to in-person school is the rapid increase in childhood anxiety and depression that has been widely noted. Reports indicate that for many reasons associated with the life changes occurring during this pandemic, suicidal ideation is up and depression and anxiety are at record highs.

As a country, we were already seeing rises in these numbers prior to the lockdown, but the number has drastically risen. Kids need to get back to life, which in many cases includes school. In the pages that follow, we will explore some of the challenges and issues that can interrupt and complicate this re-entry.

The pandemic didn't arrive in a psychological vacuum. Prior to the pandemic, trends in suburban parenting included high levels of parental involvement. This trend pulled away from the earlier laissez-faire style of parenting wherein parents didn't attend ball games and weren't aware of their child's schoolwork beyond end-of-year grades. Increasingly, this move toward involvement has become exaggerated, hence the pejorative "helicopter" or "bulldozer" parenting references that indicate a style of parenting that involves too much parental oversight.

In this environment of increased parental involvement, discomfort is to be quickly addressed, failures to be avoided. Good parenting has been confused with protecting your child from all social and academic difficulties, struggles, and failures. Families feel pressure to minimize the distress that children feel, as well as pressure to ensure that children present at their best and brightest. We don't have time for failures, as we need to always be doing our best! Plus, failure is painful, and we hate to see our children suffer.

Childhood activities have changed and often no longer involve free time to explore the world and one's limits. School refusal, relatively unheard of in our practices ten years ago, has become a daily topic of discussion. In general, a culture of "safety" has arisen. As Greg Lukianoff and Jonathon Haidt wrote in their book Coddling of the American Mind, ancient wisdom such as "what doesn't kill you makes you stronger" seems to have been lost and replaced with the assumption of fragility and "what doesn't kill you makes you *weaker*." On a regular basis, the impacts of this culture were seen in our practices, prior to the pandemic. This paradigm of good parenting equaling *more* parenting was not only present but growing.

Enter COVID! It almost seems like the perfect set up. Those early weeks of COVID were terrifying! This experience was unprecedented in our lifetimes. Safety and being cautious became a mandate. "Safetyism" became needed, wise, and required.

Gradually, as we lived with this new reality, we learned a great deal. Part of what we know now is that children and adolescents who contract COVID largely have minor or no symptoms. We better understand transmission (usually air-borne particles) and best practices to prevent transmission. Treatments have been developed and continue to improve, and finally, vaccines are here! Inevitably we will face lingering struggles such as vaccine effectiveness, mutations of the virus, and ranging immunities to the virus. All along the path, however, families have made and will continue to make decisions, with the best possible intentions, regarding the return to school.

As in-person school begins in earnest, many families will be forced to adjust to meet the new demands. In Texas, where we practice, a variety of schooling options have been available since the fall of 2020 (in-person public, online public, hybrid, and more). Based on our experiences with various families, we felt strongly that a well-presented, easy-to-read and -understand guide could be helpful for many families. We wrote this book with the hope of facilitating success for families as they face this new adventure.

CHAPTER 2

How to Use This Book

This book has been organized so that you can read it straight through or go directly to chapters of interest. We hope that parents will read the developmental stage that their child is in as well as the ones before and after. Your child may benefit from information that we elected to put into the developmental stage above or below your child. Children mature at different rates, and the developmental stages referred to represent a typical experience.

We have tried to be succinct and thus offer bullet-point lists to keep the effort needed to gain the information as low as possible. We have no desire to add to the already overcrowded schedules of most parents! The bullet-point lists offer suggestions and tips that you can add to your current repertoire of ideas. You may already be implementing some of the suggestions we make. We hope you'll find new tips as well as ways to tweak your current plans to make them more effective.

The information in this book is meant to be helpful to not only parents, but also educators, education administrators, grandparents, and other individuals who work with children. We encourage you to find relevant ideas or tips and then experiment with them to aid both yourself and your child in decreasing any anxiety or discomfort associated with returning to in-person school.

In fact, many of the topics covered here are beneficial for re-engaging in all pre-COVID activities. We've simply chosen to address school as it is a universal change that nearly all children and families will face. Hopefully, the information in this book will be helpful in other areas as well.

Being in a heightened state of caution, fear, and isolation, for over a year will have an effect on most individuals. It is natural that humans will experience some difficulties emerging from the lengthy shutdown, even when it has been so long desired. This book addresses how specific ages and groups of children may be affected. The strategies to best help each age range are slightly different. The assistance needed by special populations is also unique.

Each family entered the COVID era with characteristics that will have implications for how they exit the COVID era. Anxiety, depression, learning differences, behavioral problems, and many other factors are addressed in this book. Undoubtedly, we have overlooked some factors and will not thoroughly address every unique situation. Nonetheless, we are hopeful that the information included in this book will aid your family and the families of others to navigate these unfamiliar waters smoothly.

We encourage you to highlight, underline, write notes, or write angry responses to what we have written. Get the most out of this book as possible. You have been making decisions for your family's well-being throughout this entire COVID ordeal. This next phase, return to life, is simply the next step in taking care of your family. We suggest you consider the following:

- Read through the information or go to specific chapters.
- Scan bullet points for suggestions and tips.
- Make notes and build upon strategies you already use.
- Search for additional reading if your family situation is more severe than what is being discussed.
- Consider seeking professional help if additional reading is not helpful or if you've already exhausted those resources.
- Remember that you are not alone. Many families are facing these challenges.
- Be understanding that we have written this book in an effort to be helpful and with the best of intentions..

- Know that we are on your side. We truly want every family to find the path best for them and specifically for their children.

CHAPTER 3

General Philosophy

Y
ou should be warned that we are heavily invested in children being resilient and having the ability to persevere regardless of the situation in front of them. These qualities do not occur in a vacuum. They build over time as children experience setbacks and find a way to move forward. As with more academic learning, we can learn much from everyday mistakes.

Many parents (including us) are uncomfortable when their child is in pain or suffering in any way. Often we want to reduce their pain, reassure them, and if possible prevent bad things from happening to them. This pattern, however, can backfire and become detrimental.

There is a fine line between supporting and helping your child and hindering their progress by providing too much scaffolding. It is a constantly evolving line, one that is different for each child and for each situation.

The old adage, "Prepare the child for the path, not the path for the child," imparts great wisdom. The road of life is often challenging. Helping children to learn that they are strong and that they can cope with stressors can be very empowering for them. When they are young, sometimes we can actually sweep the path clean for them. However, we do to their detriment. The small traumas of the first grader turn into the bigger struggles of the high schooler. Victory on the small struggles builds confidence and provides the child with actual evidence that they can deal with tough situations.

Pre-COVID Scenario: Sally, a bright and active second grader, reported to her mother that her friends were bullying her and wouldn't play with her at recess. She was sad and her mother was heart-broken and frankly a bit angry. That just sounded mean! She inquired about the details of the situation. Sally reported that her best friends, Jaqui and Isa, had told her that she was too bossy. They wanted to play something at recess other than Sally's favorite, four-square. Sally's mom is good friends with Isa's mom. She immediately called Isa's mom and reported on the sad events of the day. Isa's mom was very apologetic and clearly embarrassed. She later talked with Isa and insisted that Isa be "nice" to Sally at recess.

Unfortunately, both well-intentioned moms were robbing the girls of wonderful opportunities for growth and learning. What if Sally is indeed dominating the choice of recess activities? The other girls are simply giving her some needed feedback: *take turns.* Sally may miss this important lesson because of well meant adult intervention. Worst of all, Sally now sees that her problems will require adult intervention. She has not learned that regardless of the outcome, she can deal with it, either by solving the problem with Isa and Jaqui or by finding other playmates.

To be sure, this scenario is simplified, but it's far from uncommon. Sally has been saved from short-term discomfort, but has missed out on important lessons. In addition, the term "bully" used by Sally at the outset of the scenario is not accurate in this case. Pay attention to the way that kids talk and help them to be less dramatic. While the interchange between the children may have been a bit mean, we suggest retaining the term "bully" for more serious situations.

In the chapters that follow, we encourage great empathy for kids at each phase of development. Their lives have been disrupted – or some, in completely life-altering ways! But, remember, life is constantly throwing difficult challenges our way. The "story" we want children to tell themselves as we emerge from COVID needs to be one of resilience. Be aware of the possible stressors and pitfalls of this return to life, but don't feel that you must smooth every aspect of the return.

After being isolated for lengthy periods of time, the return into crowded society can be awkward for many people. Perhaps you've noticed yourself watching movies and thinking, "Where are their masks? Why are they so close together?" Maybe you've had dreams

17

of people wearing masks or fears of uncontrollable bad things happening around you.

Many people who have had no previous anxiety or other mental health concerns will likely find themselves uneasy as personal space decreases once again and they return to togetherness. People have developed new habits to survive through the pandemic. Being around groups of other people will likely feel awkward in some situations before it feels normal again.

Many of us look forward to warm embraces from family and friends, the ability to gather with loved ones without fear, and the ability to travel, shop, vacation, and experience life without the word "virtual" attached. But some of our experiences will feel so foreign that they will become uncomfortable and we may wonder why. We have never been uncomfortable in these situations before – why now?

As difficult as readjustment may be for adults, the experience can be even more unsettling for children and adolescents. The youngest children may not be able to verbalize or even understand why they feel awkward and uncomfortable in public. Some younger children may not remember life prior to the pandemic. Older children and adolescents may be conflicted about their desire for interaction as they have either lost or not gained the year of social experience that others were able to get before COVID.

In this book we will discuss the issues that are most relevant for certain developmental stages as well as for specific populations (e.g., oppositional or anxious children). Being prepared for potential emotional struggles and discussing/addressing these with your children may help you to arm them with the power to get through any awkwardness and enjoy their ability to rejoin each other. Let's help children to see themselves as capable of coping with both COVID restrictions and the return to normal activities.

CHAPTER 4

How to Cope with Fear

Fear can be realistic or unrealistic. Unfortunately, we sometimes have difficulty distinguishing between the two. In the middle of a terrible storm with tornado warnings, we can fear a tornado as we are watching and listening to weather experts and heeding their advice. We can also fear a tornado on a clear, sunny, day continuously glancing out the window to check for storm development and checking in with weather experts about today's weather.

Realistic fear is dealt with by collecting information and problem solving. Unrealistic fear, however, is often increased by these methods. A general rule of thumb is that irrational fears are rarely calmed by rational information. Both types of fear are addressed by having awareness of and accepting the risk that something bad might happen. Perhaps the most difficult aspect of deciding how to cope with fear is determining if the fear is realistic or unrealistic.

When the fear is realistic and acute, instinctively our senses heighten so that we can assess the situation (collect information) and then determine the best course of action (problem solve). If you've ever heard a bump in the night you can recall freezing and carefully listening for additional sounds. You may have also been simultaneously considering your next move. Even when we do not do this instinctively, it is a great way to initially address the feared situation.

For many years pilots have passed down this advice to fellow pilots: "When you have an emergency, the first thing to do is wind your watch." The idea being that when a true emergency strikes you should first take a step back, take a breath, then assess the situation. After you have done this, you can identify your plan and execute it. This is excellent advice for acute fear situations, while flying and otherwise.

But what happens when the fear is unrealistic or excessive? If a person is afraid of monsters in the dark, and that fear is irrational (no monsters actually exist, at this moment, in this dark), then the fear will decrease the most when the person is exposed to being in the dark. A rational discussion that monsters are not present is not integral to the reduction of anxiety. It is more important that the person be in the dark and allow their anxiety to build, plateau, and then reduce in a process known as habituation.

Exposure to the feared situation, not avoidance, allows habituation to occur. If we escape a situation while the anxiety is building, we tend to increase the likelihood that the fear will be maintained and may grow. Not escaping, but rather staying in the uncomfortable situation, allows for habituation which disrupts the maintenance of the fear.

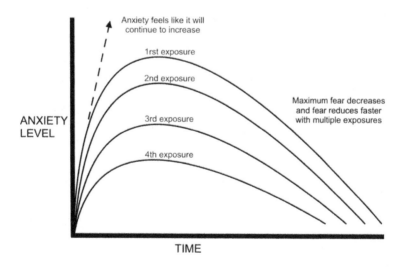

Example 1: If someone is afraid of a particular ride at an amusement park, the first ride will be terrifying. The fifteenth time they ride it that day it will likely be thrilling, but much less frightening.

Example 2: If a child is afraid of the neighbor's thirteen-year-old Labrador Retriever (very sweet and docile), running from the dog and avoiding the dog will either maintain the fear or increase the fear. Going toward the dog, eventually being able to sit near the dog, pet the dog, be beside the dog for quite some time, will result in a fear decrease. The decrease will occur regardless of whether the child is in the same room with the dog for three hours or whether the child slowly approaches the dog over three weeks.

In the previous examples, the risk to the child is present but is very low. What about situations in which the risk is present and low, but where we have less certainty about how low? As the known level of risk becomes less known or increases, more things can occur that disrupt fear reduction. However exposure remains the best initial approach.

Example 3: After getting into a small auto accident, a teen driver is likely to have some fears when driving. Not driving for the following four months is unlikely to lessen the fear. Driving, even short distances, after the accident will reduce the fear. In general, the more the teen drives, the greater the fear reduction. The best results occur when the teen driver is willingly driving and accepting some level of risk but moving ahead regardless.

Example 4: If a child is afraid of ordering their own food at a restaurant, their fear is unlikely to decrease if friends and family order for them. This avoidance serves the short term, in that the child feels much safer and happier, but they will continue to be unable to order for themself next time. The more often the child orders on their own, even if quietly or awkwardly, the fear will reduce, their skills will increase, and they will be better equipped to order on their own the next time with less distress. Great reductions in fear are seen after a great deal of practice, so you wouldn't expect greatness on the second try. Note that the fear may reduce, but the child may still dislike the experience. As most adults will agree, there are many experiences that we dislike in adulthood. The important factor is that we can do them, hopefully without undue fear.

Each of these examples demonstrates, albeit simplistically, that we reduce unrealistic and excessive fear by going *toward* the feared activity or concept. In reality, this can be incredibly difficult to do. Success decreases if we believe that the risk of the feared event is very high, if we believe that it is a realistic fear (*I am certain I will die* – we are not likely to do the activity).

Many of our fears about COVID are rational and realistic. It is a virus that has resulted in the deaths of hundreds of thousands of people in the United States alone. Some of our fears were realistic in the beginning (early March of 2020) when we had limited information and understood the virus to transmit in every possible manner and be deadly to everyone. Some of the lingering fears of COVID may be less rational or realistic.

Unfortunately, the media, the CDC, and all levels of the government have given us conflicting or misleading data such that it can be difficult to decide who and what to believe. What seems completely false and low risk to some is considered absolute truth and very high risk to others. We wish we had definitive information to give, but clearly we don't. We encourage each family to thoroughly examine the current data and be open to the idea that some fears are less realistic now that we have further information. We also encourage families to weigh the likelihood and importance of all threats. As COVID vaccines and herd immunity emerge, other threats to our well-being may take precedence. Good luck to us all!

DEVELOPMENTAL STAGES

"There is in every child at every stage a new miracle of vigorous unfolding"

— ERIK H. ERIKSON

"If you can t fly then run; if you can t run then walk; if you can t walk then crawl, but whatever you do you have to keep moving forward"

— MARTIN LUTHER KING

"We cannot always build the future for our youth, but we can build our youth for the future"

— FRANKLIN DELANO ROOSEVELT

CHAPTER 5

Kindergarten — 2nd Grade

Luckily, children ages four to eight are likely to adjust quickly to the return to the classroom from an emotional standpoint. For some children in this age group, missed educational milestones may be a bigger area of concern (see Chapter 23). With family discussion about the importance of heading back to school and following school rules, most kids in this group will pop back into the routine. In large part, kids in this age group will take their lead from parents: if parents seem relaxed and confident about the return, kids will follow.

If your child had separation anxiety or difficulty when first attending school, you may need to go through the painful separation again. You'll likely be able to use many of the strategies that you originally used, such as the use of a transition object and placing clear boundaries for when and where parents will be in the school. Childhood separation anxiety is hard on parents! To relieve some of the anxiety for parents, teachers are sometimes willing to send a quick "thumbs up" text message to indicate that the crying has stopped (often almost immediately after the parent has left the room).

The children in these grades are rather concrete in their thoughts. Developmentally, as a group, they have not fully formed abstract thinking skills. They are often very aware of what the "right and wrong" ways are to do things. They are very aware of who is following rules and who is not. It's normal for this age to be learning how to stand in line, keep their hands to themselves, and wash their hands after going to the bathroom.

Luckily, these developmental tendencies may be helpful during the return to in-person education. When teachers lay out the rules for COVID safety, children in grades K–2 are likely to understand and quite reasonably follow the rules. This has certainly been true for many of the children we work with in this age group.

Even children who are not particularly great at following the rules are usually quite aware of what the rules are! The solution is not to remove the rules, but rather to help these children by providing higher levels of structure and more frequent feedback, both positive and corrective. Children in this age range generally benefit from clear boundaries and predictable rules. Eventual compliance is the goal.

For many in this age group, the return to in-person school will be a huge relief. Developmentally, these children should be frequently moving and rarely be sitting and staring at screens. For parents who have been trying to work and manage this age group, the return to school may seem like an answered prayer! As you prepare your student to return, remember the following:

- Keep it upbeat and fun!
- Talk up the return to school, just as you would have in the past. Make the tone celebratory and enthusiastic.
- Watch your own anxiety levels. If you have worries about COVID, consider keeping those to yourself rather than burdening your returning child with concerns.
- Wake a little early if kids drag in the morning.
- Put on fun music; – you could play "beat the song" – e.g. get dressed before the song is finished.
- Plan fun breakfasts; – this could mean fun foods, fun shapes, fun bowls, fun forks and spoons, etc.
- If your child is dragging, consider a small amount of caffeine if your pediatrician approves.
- Try to have school belongings prepared the night before when possible.

- Ramp up to the return to school by returning to other daily routines such as getting up at a set time, engaging in a morning routine, etc.
- Each day for the first week or two could include a fun item (a note from mom, dad, siblings; a new pencil; new sticker).
- Spend a few minutes after school just sitting together and talking about anything; – doesn't have to be about their day.
- Some children prefer some time alone immediately after school. – Remember that they have had LOTS of alone time during the previous year and the number of people and demands upon them at school may be exhausting.
- Don't forget afternoon snacks which may help revive hungry kids, stabilize blood sugar and even build self-control reserves!
- Initially, focus more on getting into the routine than on grades!
- Make executive decisions about homework based upon your child's emotional needs, – but push them forward as soon as is reasonably possible.
- Don't forget to keep the family fun time that was special during the past year!

CHAPTER 6

3rd Grade — 5th Grade

Third grade often coincides with a cognitive leap that allows for deeper thought and more complex synthesis of information. These years often include the beginning of puberty, which may include developing external features of males and females, the all-too-pungent body odor, and increasing involvement of hormones in moods.

Although it sometimes occurs earlier, many children will have growing anxiety and worries at this time (often beginning around age nine or ten). If this anxiety or worry becomes a significant problem for your child, you may benefit from a lengthy discussion about the content of their fear (someone dying, illness, schoolwork, classmates) to better understand exactly what the focus is of the concern. This will put you in a much better position to address the anxiety.

Although you will likely offer reassurance and education to your child regarding their worries, often the best help comes from actually confronting their fears in a gentle but consistent manner. If the worries result in behavioral problems or serious impairment in functioning, consultation with a professional could be very helpful.

The kids represented in grades three to five are developing important social skills. Such a significant amount of socialization is occurring at these ages that a return to in-person classrooms will be vital to many. In early elementary school, friendships are often based on who your parents 'friends are and proximity – who is near and available. As kids enter third grade and beyond, friendships become more personal. They are based more frequently on shared interests and deeper emotional ties. Unsupervised social interaction becomes even more important during this period. Learning the rules of social relationships with peers and teachers sets the stage for further learning during the rough middle school years ahead. This is a particularly important age at which to allow your child to explore their social environment, receive feedback from their peers and other adults, and allow mistakes to be made. Some other things to keep in mind are the following:

- Review points from the "Kindergarten – 2nd Grade" chapter, as they apply to grades three to five as well.

- An important "return to school" discussion should include class rules regarding safety protocols as well as general rules (no talking, keep hands to self, be kind to others). Keep the tone light and informative.

- These grades may have a variety of digital and written homework, which may be quite confusing. Parental help to establish good habits, especially during the first weeks, may be very beneficial.

- Friendship issues can create drama that is difficult to process for children who have "lost" a year of the socialization offered by in-person school. Provide them with support as they sort through these struggles, but allow them to think through their situation as much as possible.

- Reinforce relationship concepts of empathy and setting boundaries for friends, family, and teachers.

- If your child has been particularly isolated, encourage group sports or activities and playdates when possible. Coursework in these grades tends to increase in difficulty and complexity. You may need to spend extra time with your child helping them to learn concepts or may need to locate an appropriate tutor to help them gain mastery.

- Remember that many, many children are in this same position and your child may not be uniquely behind the entire group. Rather, the entire group is behind. We want to overcome the academic losses, but we want to do so at a pace that is reasonable for each individual child. Your child may proceed faster or slower than others. It is better to be making progress in general than to be concerned with doing it overnight.

- It is just as important to foster the desiring and enjoyment of learning as it is to do the homework correctly (possibly more so).

CHAPTER 7

6th Grade — 8th Grade

Who doesn't remember the pain of these years and the social anxiety that is often inevitable? Puberty is in full swing, and everyone's body is changing at a different rate. A child in this age group has the potential to experience difficulties even if they have been attending in-person classes and will now simply be adding returning students to their world.

Gossip is frequent and friend groups may be very active on social media. It is important to note that social media is both invigorating and enlightening as well as toxic and oppressive. Limiting your child's social media exposure is not the cure-all that we'd like it to be. Children can experience the influence of social media even if they do not have direct access. In fact, some children become angry and feel unheard by their parents if denied access, which can erode the parent–child relationship and trust. We suggest an honest and clear discussion regarding family decisions on social media that takes the child's views into account. Short story: social media is a double-edged sword, particularly for this age group. It is certainly something to be monitored and considered, but its absence isn't a panacea for adolescent angst.

In addition to social media (e.g. SnapChat, Instagram, Twitter, Facebook), digital pastimes experienced by kids during the pandemic include texting, video gaming, binge-watching shows, watching TikToks, and watching YouTube videos. Screen time has entertained many. Each of these deserves family consideration for its value and time consumption.

Although a knee-jerk reaction may be to restrict each of these activities, we encourage you to consider what is best for your family and child based on research as well as social norms in your area. It might be better to opt for the middle ground rather than an all-or-none approach. There are many options available to families.

Many of the families that we see have relaxed their rules for social media during the pandemic. The return to school may provide an opportunity to regain balance if the rules have been relaxed a bit too far. This really isn't too different from reverting to an earlier bedtime when returning to school in the fall. Kids can adjust to this type of recalibration.

For some children and adolescents, the pain inflicted via social media is worsened because it is their main source of social interaction and feedback. For others, the use of screens provides a positive experience (Animal Crossing and binge-watching Psych being local favorites!). Families should consider the pros and cons of each screen activity for each child. Other things to keep in mind are as follows:

- Both digital and written homework will almost certainly be required. Individual classes may use different programs for completing and submitting work. Parental help during the first weeks may be very beneficial. If your child has things under control, by all means step back.
- Friendship issues are exponentially more important than ever before. These are the years of social learning that provide the groundwork for later years. It is important that kids experience this first hand as much as possible and be allowed to make mistakes and forgive others for mistakes.
- Be available but not overbearing, as your child may want to discuss growing feelings of love and friendship.
- Although it is easy to call it moodiness, often the emotions experienced during puberty are exaggerations of very real emotions and should not be dismissed.

- Isolation limits the child's ability to practice managing their emotions and reactions. Expect a period of adjustment during transitional times.
- Reinforce relationship concepts of empathy and setting boundaries for friends, family, and teachers.
- If your child has been particularly isolated, encourage group sports or activities and get-togethers when possible.
- This age group may have a great need for alone time. If you notice your child self-isolating once they arrive home from school, discuss their need for privacy and accommodate their needs as much as is reasonable for the family.
- Consider screen time and social media as both positive and negative. Be open to reconsidering the best limitations for your family.
- Consider developing a contract with your child to address digital rules.
- For many children, the loss of preferred screen time is a very effective strategy for motivating improved behavior or compliance with rules. Try to use punishment sparingly and positive reinforcement more generously.

CHAPTER 8

9th Grade — 10th Grade: Pre-Driver's License

These grades are filled with adolescents who are fully into their teenage years. Freshmen and sophomores are beginning their high school years and setting the stage for life beyond K–12 education. Students who have missed their freshman year of high school by being online will be at an obvious disadvantage to other students; luckily, they will learn quickly! They have so much to tackle: the layout of the building, how to navigate the lunch line, making new friends if multiple schools feed into the high school, extracurricular activities and sports, and of course high school courses, which have increased difficulty as well as increased expectations and pressure.

Adding to the frustration of this age is the growing independence that has been slowed or stopped by the pandemic – such as driving, having a job, and often making their own decisions. Adolescents in this age range may be more rebellious and more resentful of house rules that they do not believe to be fair or necessary. This lack of independence may be felt particularly intensely given the close quarters of being home with parents 24/7. Returning to in-person school may be a gift for many students (and parents)!

Early dating, or at least interest in dating, is also occurring during these years. This social experience has been radically shut down during the pandemic. These important experiences serve as practice for future romantic relationships. This is practice that will have been lost.

Integral to romantic relationships is the notion of being attractive. This perception may have accurately or inaccurately been altered during quarantine. Some kids may have taken this opportunity to "glow up" by improving their appearance during the absence. Many others may have "glowed down," having really let their appearance decline during their time in isolation. Obviously, glowing up would be the more desirable outcome, but not necessarily the more likely. The complications for kids who (rightly or inaccurately) feel that they have glowed down seem tremendous. Particularly during adolescence, when appearance is often a significant area of focus or concern, and when body changes due to puberty are the norm, it would be pretty upsetting to return to school and have your peers feel that you have let things go.

"Glowing down" seems to be a very common consequence of the pandemic. Increased access to food; reduced physical activity as screens took center stage and after school sports activities were limited; lack of access to hair salons; and decreased attention to basic hygiene – these were all real consequences of the pandemic. Kids are not immune. It might be a real deterrent to wanting to get back in the game.

In this regard, basic parental empathy and awareness of possible poor self-perception are called for. In some cases, action might be taken to help kids feel more in charge of their own bodies. Returning to prior activities is likely to provide natural remedies in this area. Again, overprotection, or giving in to the desire to not let your child face this challenge, is likely counter-productive in the long run.

Other social losses during the pandemic include special events such as hang-outs, dances, birthday parties, school sporting events, and school extracurricular competitions. These events serve to help adolescents learn how to win, how to lose, how to be assertive, and how to balance their academic, social, and home life. During these events, adolescents have real-life opportunities to choose behaviors as they develop their identity. Losing these opportunities means that they must learn to make these choices efficiently when there is less time to make corrections. It will be important to foster these social experiences once we can safely do so.

Parents should be willing to explore aspects of the lockdown that have provided them a respite from anxieties about their teens. It may be nice to have them around more, to have more control of their social interactions, to worry less about their learning to drive, etc. But these sometimes scary moves toward independence are needed for optimal development. Other things to consider are as follows:

- Try to tailor parental oversight to the needs of your child rather than the needs of you, the parent.
- It is a good time to reevaluate the house rules for their appropriateness for the adolescent. Those who have demonstrated responsibility may enjoy increased freedoms matching their proven track record.
- Remember that a child cannot be worthy of trust until the parent has offered them an opportunity to demonstrate their trustworthiness (or untrustworthiness).
- If your child is making straight A's, it is best to stop checking their grades, unless they have asked you to help them. In this case, explore their reasoning and help them build confidence.
- Be cautious of allowing parental anxiety to infringe upon your child's growing independence.

- The year of isolation is likely to make a slightly shy adolescent become painfully shy. Encourage your child to confront their fears and regain their social comfort.

- If desired, your child may want to talk with a parent or other mentor about romantic relationships and early dating do's and don'ts.

- When possible, allow your child to make their own decisions (e.g., making their own lunch or electing to buy lunch at school). If you strongly disagree with their decisions (french fries and pizza every day), take the opportunity to discuss why you would recommend a different decision. Look for compromises.

- If your child is capable of independently accomplishing something (such as waking up in the morning, getting to school without reminders, doing their own laundry), then you should pull back from oversight unless they requested it. Allow them to fall down.

- If they fall down, discuss the path forward and do not return to heavy oversight if possible. Allow your child to succeed on their own.

- You can always offer your services to remind your child that they can request help (I'm happy to remind you if you would like me to do so.).

CHAPTER 9

11th Grade — 12th Grade: Ages 16 — 19

Adolescents who have had their junior and/or senior year during 2019–2020 or 2020–2021 have been hit especially hard with lifestyle losses. These years are often a mixture of excitement, stress, eager anticipation, and intense anxiety. High-level coursework, college applications and/or decisions about the future, varsity sports and activities, leadership roles in extracurriculars, banquets, award ceremonies, prom, graduation, college visits, and college classes were all lost or compromised due to COVID.

At the exact moment that they expected to be enjoying their final years of high school, they were abruptly told to stop everything in their lives and not see any of their friends. They were told that they would be responsible for killing their parents and grandparents. Do we think that might have implications? Do we think this age group will suffer from this experience? The obvious answer is yes, but hopefully they will have pride in their survival!

Dating and the desire to date are present for many, if not most, adolescents in this age range. The pandemic may have shut down dating for some, while others have found a way. This age group, perhaps because of the uniqueness of being on the cusp of adulthood at a time when society as we know it came to an abrupt halt, is particularly frustrated.

Adolescents in these grades may vacillate between eagerness to move ahead and hopelessness about their future. COVID shutdowns have occurred along with political unrest, which may combine to create the perception that their future is doomed and that they will have too many challenges to overcome. This group is susceptible to engaging in risky behaviors, slacking or even cheating on their work, over-isolation, and/or avoiding big decisions. It is incredibly important to allow this group independence and decision making as frequently as possible, given family rules. If mistakes are made during these years, parents are present to readily help.

These are excellent years to foster good decision making which will be vital in the next years of much less parental oversight. For example, determining how much to study for an exam should be left to the child as often as possible to allow them to learn how much they, indeed, need to study. Of course, how much a parent can back away is directly related to the capability that the child has demonstrated.

These ages have growing independence and increasing awareness of the world. They are recognizing their ability to contribute to society in multiple forms. They are finding their voices and increasingly thinking about their decisions as a young adult. They may hold passionate views that they may or may not keep into adulthood; they are aware that they are a player in the game of life. Just as they began to play the game, the game was shut down. Adolescents in this age range who experience difficulty returning to in-person activities may be dealing with anxiety and stress regarding expectations placed on them by themselves or by others. Such difficulties may also indicate fears, depressed thoughts, or hopelessness regarding their future. Keep the following in mind:

- Watch for lethargy and low interest in the future.
- Emphasize the positive aspects of their future and be as flexible as possible with their future plans, such as having a Plan A, Plan B, and Plan C.
- Reinforce their independence and ability to take responsibility for themselves.

- As much as possible, decrease oversight and micromanagement to allow independence while parents are still near and can provide a safety net.
- If the student has been slacking, or even cheating, the return to in-person classes may result in greater stress and poorer grades. They may have missed important prerequisite information.
- This age group will quickly try to learn missed lessons regarding romantic relationships. This includes learning how to break up, how to be broken up with, and how to balance boyfriends/girlfriends and friends.
- Allow these students to mourn the loss of missed experiences, but try not to leave them there. Help them to reframe the crazy experiences of the past year. Help them to tell the "story" in a way that minimizes seeing themselves as victims and encourages recognition that they coped with a challenging set of circumstances.
- For some students, creative outlets may be helpful. Encourage students to journal daily about their COVID year and their observations of the return. That will be something to tell their kids about!
- Artistically bent students may find release in writing stories or plays or creating art and music that helps them to communicate about their experiences.

GENERAL FACTORS AFFECTING SUCCESS

> *"Anxiety was born in the same moment as mankind. And since we will never be able to master it, we will have to learn to live with it - just as we have learned to live with storms".*

— PAULO COELHO

> *"Inaction breeds doubt and fear. Action breeds confidence and courage. If you want to conquer fear, do not sit home and think about it. Go out and get busy".'*

— DALE CARNEGIE

CHAPTER 10

Anxious Parents

The pandemic has resulted in understandable anxiety throughout our culture. Parents, with a mission to raise children, hopefully intact, to adulthood are far from immune. Parents have been faced with multiple weighty decisions regarding how to handle the pandemic. These decisions have been complicated by a lack of reliable evidence and significant social pressure. A quick glance at any parenting group on Facebook provides plenty of contradictory opinions regarding the "proper" way to handle all of this. No wonder so many parents are anxious.

The connection between parental anxiety and child anxiety is well documented. An increase in anxiety in either the parent or the child is correlated with an increase in anxiety for the other. As more information becomes available regarding the health risks posed to children and adolescents as treatments for COVID improve, and as the vaccine becomes more widely distributed, the anxieties of many parents have been calmed. The increasing frequency of our friends, neighbors, relatives, and families 'contracting and surviving the virus also decreases anxiety, without diminishing respect for the seriousness of the virus.

For some parents, however, anxiety is not easy to vanquish. When a parent decides that it is time to return to school, it is important to remember that many of the anxieties experienced by the parent may have been transferred to the child. In order to reverse the impact of this anxiety, parents first need to gain some internal clarity and then communicate this knowledge to the kids. For some, data is calming. Familiarize yourself with the actual risk to healthy children of COVID transmission in school settings. Gather information regarding transmission rates as well as the true health risk to youths of various ages without underlying risk factors. If your child has preexisting health concerns, consult with their pediatrician or primary care physician regarding their assessment of your child's particular risks.

Unfortunately, fear and anxiety are not likely to be completely calmed by statistics. Parents may wish to think through the pros and cons of maintaining extreme caution toward COVID, especially for individuals who have either been vaccinated, have had COVID, or are not at a high risk for serious complications.

While keeping a family safe is certainly valuable, a life lived too safely could become tedious and lose meaning. At some point we would become so fearful of losing life that we'd stop living. Life is inherently dangerous. Illness has always been possible. People slip in the shower. Car crashes happen. We arm ourselves with the best information we can, we take reasonable precautions, and we forge ahead.

When it is time for your child to return to school and other aspects of pre-pandemic life, be ready to model courage for them. Remind children that courage does not mean that you do not have fear. It refers to brave actions that occur regardless of fear! Life will continue to have the risks we have always had, and we want children to learn that they can cope with these risks when they face them! When parents take this attitude, it can't help but spread to kids.

Discuss with your kids why our society made such drastic lifestyle changes and why your family feels that it is time to return to a more normal lifestyle, perhaps an even better lifestyle. For parents who suffer from anxiety, it may be challenging to communicate confidence (that is not felt) to kids. Perhaps the less anxious parent can take a bigger role in communicating with the children.

Be aware of subtle ways in which you communicate your anxiety to your child. If you are still concerned with safety, that's OK, but focus on being brave and communicating bravery to your children! Remember the following:

- Anxiety in parents can transmit to children through both genetic and environmental factors.
- Sometimes children are capable of letting go of anxiety, but their parent's anxiety prevents them from doing so. They may see the anxiety as protective (why else would Dad be that way?) or they may not want to go against the parent (Mom wouldn't like this, so I probably should not do it). While both of these are not bad parental tactics, they can amplify unnecessary anxiety.
- Pay attention to your own needs that are being met by restricting your child. Sometimes our actions are only in the interest of the child, but most often both the parent's and the child's interests are being addressed (keeps child safe, helps me sleep at night). Be aware, however, that sometimes parental actions are solely for adult benefit. Think through your decisions while identifying whose needs are being addressed.
- Seriously — Consider the consequences of restricting your child when the only needs served are your own. Mama bird is too scared and never helps her bird fly. Baby bird never flies. Never.
- Sometimes parental actions and anxiety result from pressure to be a "good parent." If all of our friends believe that

something is dangerous, then we tend to go along with their belief, even when we do not agree.

- Try to genuinely determine the best needs for your child. Sometimes that might mean being extra cautious, and other times it might mean being less cautious than other parents.

CHAPTER 11
Anxious Children

Some children seem to be anxious about almost everything. They may be described as "constant worriers." Their worries are sometimes predictable, but may often seem out of the blue. Some children are highly sensitive and very averse to change. Parents often report that these children have been anxious for as long as they can recall. A history of anxiety from a very early age may be reported by parents of children who fit this description.

Families with an anxious child have usually made efforts to reduce stressors in order to reduce their child's anxiety. Often the parents are very aware of situations and circumstances that upset their child and result in anxious meltdowns. It is very difficult to see your child in pain! So, when a parent can predict the child's pain and anxiety, it seems only logical to make attempts to shield and protect them, guarding them from discomfort.

In addition to not wanting to see a child in pain, it can also be embarrassing, frustrating, and even angering to have a child who is struggling to manage difficult emotions (melting down), especially in public. Parental shielding, which is often helpful initially, can become relied upon. Whether consciously or not, the child begins to depend on the parent to help them avoid discomfort. Simultaneously, the child loses out on opportunities to build emotional control and internal skills.

The ideal time to deal with this anxious behavior is prior to the age of five. Parents are encouraged to decrease their efforts to prevent anxiety-producing situations. When the child experiences anxiety, the parent can then help the child cope through the situation. The parent is encouraged to make a distinction between the internal experience of being uncomfortable and the external meltdown, which is a behavioral issue.

Every year after age four it becomes more difficult to make changes and the child's resulting anxiety, anger, and meltdowns will likely increase. As you can imagine, parents who were reticent to have their child experience anxiety at age four are particularly reluctant to experience the anxiety and meltdowns of their eight-, ten-, or twelve-year-old. Remember, this dynamic includes not only a child who can be anxious but also a parent who isn't sure about how to help their anxious child.

Of course, all parents shield their children from some situations: we utilize safety plugs so that children cannot electrocute themselves, we put safety locks on areas that are dangerous for children, we put the delicious-looking Tide pods out of the reach of children, we bring a snack when we know they'll be hungry, we have them take a jacket when it is cold. It is a reasonable and good thing for parents to anticipate some of their child's needs and help them learn to care for themselves.

Example: When your child is four you bring a snack for your child to eat after playtime at the park. When your child is eight you may ask your child to choose their snack and put it in the bag for after playtime in the park. When your child is ten you may suggest they get a snack if they would like one, and beyond that you may not offer any reminders at all, depending upon the child. We help children to build competence by providing decreasing levels of assistance as they mature.

But the anxious child presents special challenges. Their worrying suggests that they don't understand the likelihood of bad outcomes, and parents often use these instances as teaching moments. Again, this is more acceptable prior to age four. If an older child has unrealistic or exaggerated fears and is within normal intelligence, not understanding the risk is rarely to blame.

Parents should keep in mind that not all anxiety is bad. Anxiety is a normal human emotion. The goal is not to eliminate any experience of anxiety. Rather it is to help children recognize anxiety when it is a useful "stop sign" or "warning signal" and to be able to face anxiety that is excessive. This distinction is not always easy.

Helping the anxious child learn how to self-soothe or face their fears can be particularly difficult. The general idea is that the child must face their fears to overcome them, and the fears associated with returning to school, whether due to COVID, general germs, social issues, or other concerns, are no different. If you believe that your child's experience of fear is too difficult to tackle on your own, reach out to a professional for support. The professional will not "fix" your child but should be able to help both you and your child find better success. Keep the following in mind as well:

- Normalize any "normal" anxiety your child may be experiencing.
- Try to reframe the situation into one of coping and function versus one of dysfunction. *This will be terrible. I can t handle it!* changes to *I m nervous, but I m going to try anyway!*
- Celebrate successes in the same way. *It was a terrible day!* changes to *Parts of the day were not good, but I got through it, and some moments weren t that bad!*
- Read stories to children about facing anxiety. Point out that most "heroic" characters in popular tales experience fear and anxiety, but face it rather than running away.

- Help children understand that bravery doesn't mean that you aren't scared or anxious; it means that you face your fears anyway. Help your child be able to see themselves as brave!

- When you can, help your child avoid using anxiety as an excuse. Certainly, we may change our plans or make some accommodations for anxiety, but try to keep changes limited and reserved for emergencies.

CHAPTER 12

Oppositional Behavior

There are two types of oppositional behavior we will address. The first is oppositional behavior that occurs in conjunction with anxiety. The second is oppositional behavior that exists on its own and may pretend to be anxiety. Both are parenting challenges!

Oppositional behavior that co-occurs with anxiety can often simply look like very bad anxiety. When parents describe this type of "anxious" child, they often note that sometimes it feels a bit manipulative. This most often occurs when the child has successfully avoided anxiety-provoking situations and when parents have felt powerless against meltdowns. Children will recognize that they can escape anxiety-provoking situations fairly easily by magnifying their distress.

Secondary gain is a concept that refers to an advantage (something you gain) that is secondary to the original illness. Anxiety can have the secondary gain of attention from loved ones, avoidance of unpleasant situations, extra cuddles from parents, and special treats. Secondary gain from anxiety can include all of the positives that come from having anxiety. Of course the anxiety itself is terrible, but there are often experiences secondary to the anxiety that are quite reinforcing.

Example 1: The pandemic has offered unlimited secondary gain for children and adolescents with social anxiety. Not only do they have full permission to withdraw from society, but it has been mandated! It is fully sanctioned to not attend school, not get a job, and not interact with others. No one will even ask you to do so. Children and adolescents in this position will have a very rude wake-up call when it is time to return to school, as well as to life. They will lose their secondary gain.

Example 2: A child who was unhappy at school before the pandemic found great secondary gain with school shutdowns. Whether their anxiety was affiliated with coursework, classmates, teachers, getting up in the morning, or any other reason, they immediately were able to avoid these things when school became virtual. Upon return to school, they will experience not only the addition of anxiety but also the loss of the benefit that they experienced as the secondary gain.

Example 3: A child who experiences anxiety about non-school issues and has had a reduction of anxiety symptoms since staying home is experiencing a secondary gain of reduced anxiety and perhaps the enjoyment of staying in pajamas all day, frequent access to enjoyable activities such as playing games and taking breaks on their own schedule. We can all understand how difficult it may be for this child to return to school

In each of these examples of secondary gain, the child may engage in oppositional behavior to avoid returning to school. They may report radically increasing anxiety such that they "simply cannot" return. They may become angry or even violent and try to manipulate the situation to allow for staying at home even when it is clearly not beneficial for the student and/or family.

To address this resistance, be aware that your child likely has mixed feelings about returning to school. Yes, they would like to avoid anxiety, and, yes, they are enjoying many aspects of being home, but heading back to in-person classes also has some positives. Your child may not be able to verbalize their confusion, and anxiety may be winning, but you can help them to see the benefits of overcoming the anxiety by going through it. Keep the following in mind:

- Understand that the situation is likely more complex than simple anxiety.

- Help your child recognize what secondary gain has occurred during the pandemic (for many adults, the lack of a commute has been a glorious happenstance!).

- Discuss ways to achieve "gains" while going toward the anxiety (while returning to school).

- As needed, review the family rules for oppositional behavior (e.g., tantrums are not acceptable, but you can go to your room and be upset if needed).

- Discuss the rationale for losing the secondary gain to improve other aspects of their and their families 'lives (such as educational goals, socialization, opportunities).

- Once you have addressed the secondary gain, address the anxiety that was primary. Review the points from the previous chapter regarding the anxious child.

The second type is outright oppositional behavior with or without anxiety. Some kids use the term "anxiety" when they actually mean "I don't want to." They do this because it has worked for them. The tendency for parents to rescue children from uncomfortable experiences that are upsetting is such a natural response. It's also natural that children learn this pattern and take advantage of it when they choose. Some children may be so invested in their efforts that they, themselves, believe that their anxiety is too much to handle. Most children, however, have at least partial awareness that their anxiety is an effective tool to get what they want.

Example 1: A twelve-year-old girl doesn't want to go to school. She knows that both parents work and cannot be late. She moans all morning because school is difficult and she refuses to get ready for school. Her parents are busy getting themselves ready, and by the time they have to leave, the girl is still in her pajamas. The parents leave her home. She happily enjoys her morning, gets further behind in school work, and has more reason to hate school.

Example 2: A ten-year-old girl doesn't want to go to school and is verbally disrespectful to her mother. Father makes disparaging remarks toward Mother and doesn't correct the daughter when she copies him. Father leaves early for work and the mom is in charge of getting their daughter to school. The girl claims that she can't go to school because her mother has not provided clean clothes for her. She doesn't attend school that day. The girl wants to go to gymnastics after school but argues and throws things at the mother. Her mother rushes to get her there on time. The mom indicates that she could have chosen not to take her but believes that the commitment made to the team is more important. The daughter knows that the family has spent a great deal of money for her to be on a competitive team.

Example 3: A fifteen-year-old boy, with no history of anxiety disorder, has enjoyed schooling from home. He is bright and able to complete most of his work efficiently, leaving ample time for his true love, gaming. At times, he is even able to game during "classes." His family decides that it is time to return to in-person school. The youth claims that he is far too worried about COVID to return. He becomes emotional, and his parents are a bit overwhelmed by his apparent emotion because this is not typical of him. The parents relent, indicating that returning to school next semester will be fine.

In each of these examples, you can see the manipulation. In some of the examples, the child used the word "anxiety" as an excuse for avoiding things they do not want to do, as well as an excuse for bad behavior. In other examples, the child simply says "no" without invoking claims of anxiety. The parents respond by making choices that unfortunately maintain these bad habits.

Before we judge these parents as "bad parents" we must recognize how easy it is to see that others are giving in to the manipulation of their child and how hard it is to see it in ourselves. We should also recognize how easy it is to confuse good parenting with never letting your child experience discomfort. Many parents have capitulated to bad behavior because they did not want to make the situation "worse" for their child. In fact, at times in our office, parents seem relieved to hear that it is acceptable and actually valuable to set limits for their child who is being oppositional. Such parents often feel that they will damage their child if they are not perfectly calm and accommodate their child's emotions.

Another factor associated with oppositional behavior is motivation. It is not uncommon for a parent to be motivated to change a behavior, while the child has little or no motivation for change. This doesn't seem too surprising, really. Parents generally have a mature perspective and know what is best for kids when kids don't always understand. Consider phone use, bedtime limits, curfews, chores, homework, etc. Returning to school following COVID will fit into this category for some families. The parent sees the need, but the child prefers to stay at home. In a way, COVID has created a new problem for many families that simply didn't exist before. It has raised the possibility that in-person school attendance is optional.

In situations where the motivation for change originates with the parent, the parent must take the lead. This does not mean ignoring your child's feelings. When talking to parents who are in this challenging situation, it is often revealed to us that the parent is in much more distress than the child. Our suggestion might be that the distress needs to be transferred to the child. The reason for this is not to torture children, but rather that motivation for change is typically born of distress.

We want to make changes because the current situation is not desirable. If all of the motivation for change is with the parent, then the children, understandably, won't be motivated to make changes for themselves. This means that parents may need to alter circumstances so that the child is not so comfortable. For example, if a youth is spending excessive time on video games or social media, make enjoyment of these pleasures contingent upon desired outcomes.

Example: A thirteen-year-old girl became frustrated and yelled obscenities at her parents and siblings. Despite her behavior, she expected the parents to help her with homework and drive her to extracurricular activities at her beck and call. In addition, she did not want to attend in-person school because it was a "waste of her time" and her friends were not planning to return yet. The parents, who were very distressed, wanted her to stop yelling at them. She, who was not distressed, wanted them to get over it and accommodate her wishes.

To transfer the distress, the parents were encouraged to make their ability to help with homework and to drive her places contingent upon her not yelling or cursing at the parents and siblings. The parents were less distressed after setting this new boundary, while she was quite distressed that they weren't giving in to her demands. She became much more motivated to negotiate a fair deal with her parents. With a bit of success, the parents felt better able to insist that return to school was not optional. Keep the following in mind:

- Oppositional behavior generally refers to behaviors done in defiance of authority.
- Sometimes anxiety accompanies oppositional behavior and sometimes it does not (although the child might report anxiety as part of their oppositionality).
- Discuss with your child/adolescent that although they feel anxious, this does not excuse misbehavior. This is true for meltdowns and temper tantrums, of course, but is especially true for endangering themselves or others either physically or emotionally.

- Oppositional behavior has been linked in the literature to "strong-willed" children. Regardless of the will of the child, it is clearly an indication that the current rules for behavior and their implementation are not working for this particular child.

- Any behavior that is particularly destructive or threatening of bodily harm should be taken very seriously and not be tolerated. Seek professional help if needed. Family members, especially siblings, should not feel in danger.

- When oppositional behavior continues after parents have intervened and set limits on the behaviors, consultation with a professional may be needed.

SPECIFIC POPULATIONS: ISSUES THAT CAN AFFECT SUCCESS

"You may not control all the events that happen to you, but you can decide not to be reduced by them".

— MAYA ANGELOU

"Every student can learn, just not on the same day, or the same way".

— GEORGE EVANS

CHAPTER 13

Attention Deficit Hyperactivity Disorder

ADHD is characterized primarily by a combination of inattention to mundane tasks requiring focus and overactive/impulsive behavior. These symptoms are typically present at an early age and result in impairments in academic performance and/or social functioning. According to the DSM-5, there are three primary subtypes of ADHD. About 80 percent of children diagnosed with ADHD meet criteria for "combined" type, which includes inattention, impulsivity, and overactivity. (Just a note: The current diagnostic nomenclature doesn't include ADD. What was previously called ADD is now called ADHD, Predominantly Inattentive presentation.)

ADHD presents challenges for education even in the best of times. Simply put, it is difficult to manage on the best of days and in the best of circumstances.

While in their home environment during the shutdown, many parents have had massive struggles trying to manage children with problems in this area. Children with ADHD are often very active. They prefer hands-on activities, need frequent breaks, and often must have high levels of external structure and activity to perform well.

When the parent needs to be doing other activities, such as their own work, maintaining this structured and active type of environment can be very challenging, if not impossible. When you feel like you can't leave your child unattended for more than ten minutes (or two minutes), everyone in the household can become frustrated leading to fights and/or giving up on the work.

Depending upon the severity of the inattention and hyperactivity, online school may have led to some very bad habits that will be difficult to break once in-person school begins. Parents may have made decisions, in an attempt to survive, that will backfire later, – such as allowing extra-long breaks, doing some (or all) of the child's work, and giving in to the child's misbehavior. Siblings may also be affected by either demanding the same allowances or simply being disrupted every time their sibling is disruptive.

In an effort to contain the chaos, parents may have allowed more screen time than usual. Managing screen time for a child with ADHD can be a living nightmare for parents! While kids with ADHD have difficulty with focus, this difficulty does not extend to activities that the child finds intrinsically motivating. In fact, it is not uncommon for kids with ADHD to hyperfocus on activities that they enjoy.

Hence, children with ADHD often love some screen experiences and hate others. Alas, it is often the educational screen activities that are disliked and the recreational screen activities that are loved. Again, these kids often need movement, hands-on learning, and high levels of stimulation. Developmentally, all elementary kids need movement, but this is especially true for children with ADHD. For these young children, this may be particularly challenging during the pandemic, especially while parents are overwhelmed with their own work and monitoring the work of other children.

Example: An eight-year-old boy, who was diagnosed with ADHD prior to COVID, is attending school online. His parents are both working from home. The parents have made attempts to maintain as much routine as possible. The boy has a reasonable bedtime, and each school day they get ready for school, just as they did prior to the pandemic. After the boy is set up at his computer, the parents each step into another room where they can work. When they check on the boy, he is almost always off task, usually playing Minecraft or watching YouTube streamers. They quickly recognize that he is not completing his work on his own.

In this scenario, both parents and child are faced with a situation that is frankly untenable. From a developmental perspective, this boy is not equipped to exert the self-control needed to work on school tasks rather than enjoy immediately available and more desirable activities. The parents, however, are in a bind because they must work in order to pay the bills.

Second-grade boys are meant to play outside, touch science experiments, high five friends, and move about the school. Add ADHD at an age when exploration and sensation seeking are often high, and the problem worsens. These kids may be oppositional because it works. They get to do things that they want to do rather than stare at a screen to learn grammar.

In general, most children with ADHD are likely to be poorly served by distance learning options. The best solution, for many, will be to get them back to in-person school as soon as possible.

To aid in the transition back to in-person school, consider the following:

- Explore software that places limits on what the child can access on their computer.
- Consider hiring a tutor to structure learning.
- Consider setting up the child's work station within sight of the parent.
- For homework, consider allowing small groups to work together so that they can motivate one another. This should be viewed as a luxury, and hopefully the group will be

motivated to stay on task rather than distract each other and thus lose the privilege.

- Set limits and consequences for off-task behavior.
- Provide ample amounts of time to play outside. Insist on vigorous exercise, especially for younger children.

CHAPTER 14

Specific Learning Disorder with Impairment in Reading (Dyslexia)

For kids with reading disorders, the loss of instructional time during the pandemic raises extra concerns. In kindergarten and first grade, the foundations for solid reading skills are being laid. Early identification of reading problems is crucial because research indicates that instruction is most effective during the time frame prior to the completion of third grade.

Dyslexia is a developmental learning disorder that is characterized by underlying problems with a skill called phonological awareness. Phonological awareness refers to the ability to "play" with the sounds of oral language. Dyslexics also may have difficulty with a skill called rapid automatic naming, or RAN.

RAN tasks require a child to quickly name numbers, letters, colors, or shapes displayed on a page. Children who struggle to quickly retrieve this information may also struggle to retrieve words and phonemes. Early signs of dyslexia include difficulty learning the letter names and associated sounds.

During this COVID year, some children in this age group will have lost out on early reading instruction. This loss will make it particularly challenging to determine whether the delay in skills is due to lack of instruction or a genuine learning problem. It could be that children are behind on learning information such as letter names and sounds simply because of limited instruction and practice. It will be a true challenge to separate lack of instruction from developmental dyslexia.

Reading experts have cautioned for years that it is unwise to delay intervention or take a "wait and see" approach. In fact, for over twenty years, reading experts have strongly recommended intervention for struggling early readers, even when it is unclear that a diagnosable disorder is present. This remains good advice. As children return to school, it is important to begin intervention immediately for those in early elementary school (especially first and second grades) who are behind.

It is important that you don't delay providing assistance until a diagnosis is obtained. Instead, we suggest that intervention begin for any child who has delayed reading skills. For many, it will become clear that the early reading delays are the result of lost instruction time and can be quickly remediated. This suggests that a reading disorder such as dyslexia is not present.

Schools are often a first line of defense for helping young children who are struggling with early reading. In the fall of 2021, however, common sense suggests that schools might be overwhelmed. If your early elementary school child is struggling with reading, don't delay intervention. Talk with educators.

Public schools have a three-tiered system aimed at providing augmented instruction at the first sign of a problem. In this system, Tier 1 is general education. If a student is struggling in a particular area, they can be moved to Tier 2, which involves more intensive and small-group instruction. This intervention will not be as intense as a dyslexia program, but will increase attention to early reading.

Tier 2 doesn't require that the student be diagnosed with a disorder or disability. If a student responds well to Tier 2 intervention and their skills are normalized, then return to regular education is warranted. However, if a student continues to struggle, movement to Tier 3 might be needed.

If your child is struggling, consider asking your child's teacher about this option. Parents can always request an evaluation. But be aware, schools are likely to be overwhelmed with requests for evaluation in the wake of COVID. This will lead some parents to consider private evaluation.

When talking to schools, it has generally been our experience that, like most human interactions, a respectful, positive approach is best. When we approach school personnel, our assumption is that educators are eager to help children. We also try to keep in mind that they might be overwhelmed. If a friendly initial approach proves to be unsuccessful, it may be time to seek an educational advocate.

An obvious benefit of school intervention is its low, usually nonexistent, cost. Another benefit is that the intervention occurs during the school day. Most children learn best during the daytime when they are fresh. By the end of a long school day, kids are tired, and extensive tutoring sessions may be hampered by fatigue.

This fatigue may be particularly problematic for dyslexic children who are struggling throughout the school day. They are often exhausted. Struggling with reading for an early elementary school child is a bit like attending a calculus class without knowing addition and subtraction.

External tutoring may be your primary option if your school does not provide adequate resources. You may also choose tutoring with a reading specialist as a supplement to the school's intervention.

Both school intervention and tutoring will be guided by a wealth of research on reading issues.

Remediation of reading problems, primarily dyslexia, has a clear intervention path. Children who are struggling generally benefit from as much 1:1 and small-group instruction as possible. Reading programs that are phonics based and provide multisensory instruction have been shown to be incredibly helpful.

In general, children with reading difficulties need to read more. Trying to find reading material that is appropriate to the child's reading level and also interesting can be a challenge. Teachers, fellow parents, librarians, internet searches, and even other children may be able to offer suggestions for interesting reading material.

Additional reading during the summer months is an excellent opportunity to improve reading skills. Intensive summer reading programs, which have always been a good option, may be ideal for children who are struggling with reading during the pandemic, regardless of a formal diagnosis. Keep the following in mind:

- Although many children will be academically behind, those with learning differences are at particular risk.
- Beginning intervention based on observed weaknesses is ideal. Don't wait for a diagnosis; address reading delays as soon as possible.
- Be aware of the child's motivation to study and focus. With the changes to online coursework, there have been changes to motivation. Children may have had a much easier or a

much more difficult time. Try to motivate them for the change to in-person education.

- Consider tutoring or an executive functioning coach if you need intervention in addition to what the school is able to provide.

- Consider a variety of reading materials to match interest and skill level. Comics, graphic novels, differing genres, books with engaging pictures, and children's magazines may offer potential reading material.

- Be aware that your child is being asked to make many adjustments quickly and that the effort required from them is greater than that for other kids. Be empathetic and understanding, but maintain the expectations.

CHAPTER 15

Autism Spectrum Disorder

For individuals with Autism Spectrum Disorder (ASD), hallmark features include difficulties with social interaction/perception and difficulties with change. Secondary struggles with attention, anxiety, and oppositional behavior are not uncommon. In addition, many kids with ASD diagnosis are very keen to be online, playing games, watching YouTube, etc. These factors combined could make return to school quite challenging.

Because of these factors, many children with ASD will also benefit from returning to school. From a social perspective, exposure to good social modeling from peers is valuable. In addition, teachers often provide feedback to parents and children about what type of social errors they observe. These observations lead to guidance for treatment targets and improved social functioning.

Academic functioning for this group of children and teens varies widely. Some ASD students are very academically inclined and may not have any particular academic struggle upon return to school. Others have a range of difficulties (executive functioning weaknesses, comorbid learning problems, ADHD, etc.) and may struggle as they return to in-person school. For these students, the return to in-person special education opportunities will be very valuable.

Many children with ASD suffer from anxiety when encountering changing or new situations. Helping these students find ways to manage the unpredictability of typical in-person school will lead to improved flexibility and/or improved ability to develop routines to "appear" more flexible. Facing these changes that occur with regular in-person school will likely decrease current anxiety as well as future anxiety. Life is filled with changes, and these pupils need practice dealing with the vicissitudes of life.

Children with ASD are susceptible to heavy technology usage. This issue is, of course, a problem for many children without ASD as well. Parents often ask about how to get the child who appears to be "addicted" to video games off their devices which is not an easy task by any means.

The excessive downtime during this shutdown, often accompanied by boredom, has made this problem exponentially worse. Of course, limit setting and other strategies are needed. But, returning to school is one of the very best strategies!

Once back in the classroom, there are simply fewer hours in the day during which being online is possible. You can't be on a device twenty-four hours a day when at least seven are spent in school. For many, the reduction in hours on their devices will be difficult and many kids will get in trouble at school because they sneak onto a game or website during educational hours. But those struggles can be dealt with as needed.

The school can become an ally to parents who are fatigued with keeping track of computer use. It might be a lovely respite to have another adult providing some of the limits needed in this area. Particularly for students with ASD, school has the potential to offer many beneficial, therapeutic results.

The following suggestions may be useful for this group of students:

- Consider early introductions to teachers via video chat, especially for young children.
- Visit the school prior to the first "meet the teacher" day to familiarize your student with the environment.
- Discuss what a typical school day will be like and what might be expected. Review with your child who they might contact if something goes wrong.

- Contact the school prior to the student's return to inquire about developing an academic and/or social accommodate-ions plan.
- Review the daily schedule and help the child visualize their day. Discuss changes that might naturally occur (especially for lunch and recess or P.E.).
- If the child is particularly invested in a video game or other digital activity, discuss the changes in accessibility that will occur and when, and under what circumstances, they will be given access (such as after school, after homework, or after getting ready for bed).

CHAPTER 16

Social Anxiety

Individuals with social anxiety have excessive fears that others will judge or evaluate them negatively. The possible scrutiny from others is dreaded, and the fear of humiliation or embarrassment often leads to the avoidance of social situations. For such individuals, COVID has offered some temporary relief. The instructions to stay away from other people and to avoid leaving home have likely been welcome advice.

Anxiety levels in this group may have declined as COVID isolation has offered a brief respite from anxiety-provoking social interactions. It has also provided a respite for parents who feel that they must push their child into social experiences. Under the restrictions from COVID, social experiences have been on hold and parents have had a break from their child's unhappiness at being asked to engage socially.

Unfortunately, socially anxious children and their families will possibly have the most difficult time readjusting to life and school. They have had sanctioned avoidance of their feared situations. Avoidance as a response to anxiety, however, is an ineffective strategy. Interventions for anxiety almost always involve some form of exposure to the feared situation, something these children have not had for over a year.

When avoidance is the primary coping strategy, anxiety tends to ironically increase. Anxiety says, "Well, if school is too scary, you should probably avoid the grocery store, where you might have to interact with a clerk. And while you are at it, going for walks might result in crossing paths with other humans, so you should stay home."

Fear grows if we avoid. The saying, "If you fall off a horse, get right back on." refers specifically to fear increasing if you do not quickly confront it following a trauma. Anxiety is greedy and will want to take more of a person's life. As socially anxious kids isolate, their social skills (often mildly weak to begin with) become rusty. Emerging from quarantine will be challenging for this group of children.

Facing social anxiety is a very difficult task. For children with some social deficits, it might be helpful to review social skills as well as conduct some role-playing activities before returning to in-person classes. For all individuals with social anxiety, gradual exposure to social situations and the potential for negative evaluation should be considered. You may begin with family gatherings or by going into small stores and work up to larger stores and more exposure to peers.

For good or bad, our society has made it increasingly easy to avoid social situations. Food and goods can be delivered, you can communicate with friends and family online, and so many activities can be done remotely. It is easy to see that if a child has no motivation to overcome their fears they will have no motivation to enter anxiety-provoking situations.

Parents, however, can recognize that this avoidance will shut doors of opportunity for their child and are often highly motivated for their child to be more interactive. Motivating the socially anxious child, however, is a great challenge. This is particularly true for the child refusing to attend school.

Prior to the pandemic, school refusal had become a rather common presenting problem in our practice, not just for young children, but also for kids throughout childhood and adolescence. During COVID, school refusal as a presenting problem became less prevalent.

Some children, however, refuse to participate in online school, especially when they must be on camera. As more schools reopen, and more parents decide that returning to in-person education is the best choice for their families, expect school refusal to increase.

Parents are encouraged to discuss their rationale for the importance of returning to in-person classes, despite the social pressures. Depending upon the age of the child, they may offer incentives for attending school without fussing. In cases of more severe social anxiety, professional help and even medications often prove to be beneficial.

Keep the following in mind:

- Check in on the social skills of socially anxious kids and help them "brush up" in areas where they may have become a bit rusty.
- Provide kids with some thoughts on how to begin conversations with open-ended questions.
- Encourage socially anxious kids to be curious about other people and focus less on themselves.
- Provide your child with practice opportunities (e.g., making phone calls, ordering in restaurants, talking with clerks).
- Encourage your child or adolescent to set goals of casual interactions (e.g., say hello to two people, ask one person how their weekend was, nod hello to 2 people, answer a question from the teacher, ask the teacher a question).

- Consider reading some self-help books on social anxiety. There are options available for different age ranges.
- Discuss the acceptability of introversion (which can be associated with social anxiety). Introversion is a perfectly acceptable character trait; social anxiety paralyzes people and hinders their ability to live successfully.
- Encourage your child or adolescent to be less judgmental of others as well as themselves, and to expect that others should cut them slack as well. Everyone makes errors or blunders, and we should forgive them when they do, forgive ourselves when we do, and expect them to also forgive us when we do.
- Anxiety is an explanation but not an excuse.
- Avoidance has a strong tendency to increase anxiety and fear. Avoidance is a short-term strategy, whereas exposure therapy is a long-term strategy to address anxiety.
- Usually social anxiety does not dissipate on its own. It may lessen with age, but it is likely that age requires us to participate more. So, perhaps it is less of a maturation benefit and more of an exposure benefit.

CHAPTER 17

Health/Illness Anxiety

S ome people had excessive concerns about their health long before COVID. Health anxiety, as discussed here, simply refers to the excessive, unrealistic concern that something is wrong with the person's health. This anxiety may result in repeated checking for symptoms and seeking reassurance through additional means, such as doctor visits, googling symptoms, and asking the opinions of others.

You might think that anyone with health anxiety has had a particularly difficult time with COVID (a true health risk). Many, however, have not been overly concerned with COVID itself but have still had difficulties. In particular, because individuals with health anxiety often seek reassurance through doctor visits, the lack of non-essential doctor visits due to the shutdown has likely been frustrating.

Other individuals with health anxiety are completely overwhelmed by COVID and fear that every symptom is a COVID symptom. It certainly hasn't helped that the news is constantly reporting "new COVID symptoms" that include basically everything. Currently, the media is reporting new long-term symptoms that are likely to also exacerbate health anxiety.

Many people without health anxiety have reported an increase in self-checking for symptoms and fears that those symptoms indicate COVID. It makes sense that someone who has a history of excessive health concerns could truly spiral out of control with COVID. The pandemic has increased hypervigilance to health and illness symptoms for everyone!

Children and adolescents with health anxiety (both related to COVID and not related) may have difficulties returning to school as the general discussion of health symptoms is ubiquitous. This constant discussion is likely to create additional anxiety, which can sometimes cause paralyzing panic attacks and difficulty with focus on schoolwork.

The good news is that by simply returning to school, the health anxious child will naturally participate in exposure therapy. To keep them from school would likely result in anxiety growth, as avoidance usually does. Another positive note is that returning to school serves as exposure therapy for every student, and classmates will soon decrease their discussion of symptoms.

If your child experiences crippling anxiety that is not improving, we suggest consulting a professional to help create a plan for going forward. To aid the reduction of health-anxiety symptoms, the following suggestions may be helpful:

- Encourage children and adolescents to limit Google searches on health symptoms. Rather than offering reassurance, such searches often result in increased anxiety and more fears.
- Encourage your child to take a wait-and-see approach. If they experience a symptom and want to seek reassurance, they are encouraged to wait and see if it worsens; while they wait they should try to engage in alternative activities. Continuing to think about the symptoms does not count as waiting.
- If your child is obsessive over health concerns, try to approach symptoms in a nonchalant manner. Try not to give symptoms much concern as you model the wait-and-see approach. Help your child focus on something else as you wait.
- Avoid providing excessive reassurance. Discuss with your child that reassurance offers poor short-term relief without any long-term relief. The next symptoms will create the same amount of anxiety.

- A child who is of at least average intelligence should be reassured no more than one time. If your child is seeking reassurance repeatedly, this suggests an obsessive quality to their health anxiety.

- Consider discussing with your child the strength of the immune system and how it is further strengthened through "stress." Even this discussion should only be done once or twice if you believe that your child is becoming obsessive over health concerns.

- Anxiety is an explanation but not an excuse.

- Maintain the expectation of courage and behavioral control (i.e., no meltdowns or outbursts that disrupt others) regardless of the anxiety the child is experiencing.

- Some helpful anxiety-reducing strategies include meditation, deep breathing, and journaling. There are some very good self-help guidebooks that your child may find helpful. The strategies, however, are most useful in conjunction with exposure therapy wherein the child faces their fears and feared situations.

- Avoidance has a strong tendency to increase anxiety and fear. Avoidance is a short-term strategy whereas exposure therapy is a long-term strategy to address anxiety.

CHAPTER 18

Obsessive Compulsive Issues

Obsessive Compulsive Disorder is characterized by obsessions (intrusive thoughts, images, or impulses) and compulsions (internal or external efforts to reduce the obsession). OCD is often focused upon the fear that something catastrophic will occur due to something that the person has or has not done.

Compulsions often include checking and reassurance seeking, doing something repetitively, or doing things in a certain way to prevent something bad from happening. These compulsions can be external (e.g., checking a lock, confessing) or internal (e.g., going over something in their head, saying certain things or prayers).

Although OCD can be primarily focused upon health and somatic issues (discussed in the previous chapter), it can also be focused on many other things and can take many forms. Children and adolescents with OCD may not have suffered much more than usual during COVID shutdown and may actually have felt freed by not attending class or other activities. Because they have been successfully avoiding their OCD triggers, these kids may be reluctant to return to in-person education.

OCD presents a special problem following the shut down. OCD may have worsened while home, making it more difficult to return to school; OCD may have lessened while home, making it more difficult to return to school. Luckily, either way, OCD has a high potential of improving following the return to school.

If symptoms worsened while at home, going to school will provide a structured environment that can lessen OCD symptoms. If symptoms have decreased due to avoidance, returning to school serves as exposure therapy, which is likely to result in further symptom reduction. If symptoms have decreased due to a decrease in general stressors, then we suggest that the family discuss ways to maintain the lowered stress level regardless of return to school. Professional consultation may help if the anxiety from OCD continues to escalate or is paralyzing.

As your child or adolescent with OCD returns to school and other activities, the following suggestions may be helpful:

- Anxiety is an explanation but not an excuse.
- Be understanding and empathetic to their fears but maintain the expectation of courage and behavioral control (i.e., no meltdowns or outbursts that disrupt others).
- OCD does not usually resolve on its own. The symptoms tend to increase and decrease, waxing and waning, over a lifetime. Sometimes symptoms increase due to stressors, but other times increases seem random. Most consistent symptom reductions are associated with (formal or informal) exposure therapy and/or medication.
- Recognizing OCD or simply obsessive anxiety that doesn't meet criteria for OCD is important. Being able to identify that it is an obsession that is raising the fear can help differentiate typical fears from OCD fears.
- Some helpful anxiety-reducing strategies include meditation, deep breathing, and journaling. There are some very good self-help guidebooks that your child may find helpful. The strategies, however, are most useful in conjunction with exposure therapy wherein the child faces their fears and feared situations.
- Avoidance has a strong tendency to increase anxiety and fear. Avoidance is a short-term strategy, whereas exposure therapy is a long-term strategy to address anxiety.

- If the child's anxiety does not decrease or is worsening, seeking professional help, including therapy and/or medications, may be beneficial.

CHAPTER 19

Depression Issues

The main symptom of depressive disorders is generally depressed mood. Depressed individuals often feel hopeless or guilty, are anxious, lack energy, and struggle to concentrate. Lack of interest in previously enjoyed activities is often present.

For some people, depression is significant and results in an inability to function. For others, depression is mild but chronic and may have lasted for years. For yet others, depression may be very severe and can even be associated with brief psychosis or suicidal ideation. Some children and adolescents were suffering prior to COVID, but many others have become depressed during the pandemic.

We don't know how many kids were going to be depressed this year, regardless of COVID, and how many are unique cases caused by COVID and its fallout. This has also been a time of political unrest and uncertainty, which may contribute to mood declines and feelings of hopelessness.

Returning to in-person school may greatly help these children. Anything that begins to normalize life will likely help moods. There will be some, however, who are now in a depressed state that will not improve easily. Signs to look for include isolation, lack of initiative, irritability, lack of self-care, lack of enjoyment or interest, feelings of guilt or shame, and, of course, depressed mood.

The isolation that has been imposed upon children and adolescents is unprecedented. Some children have been lodged for the past year with unhealthy family situations. Most people can recognize that an abusive family member would make for an unhealthy family situation, but many other environments also qualify as unhealthy.

Some examples include contentious parents; divorcing parents; sibling discord; having one or both parents impaired by depression, anxiety, or other mental illness; overbearing parents; substance abuse in the home; and negligent parents. Family togetherness is not always calming and joyous.

Even with an ideal family unit, the isolation and confinement imposed during the shutdown can be associated with depressed mood. In addition to family matters contributing to mood, the peer group, or lack thereof, also contributes. Peers have always been an important factor in the lives of children and adolescents. Peers are important in everyone's lives. During the shutdown, however, our access to peers has been radically changed.

Some friends were shut down completely and may not have had internet access, while others were allowed to have sleep-overs. For some kids, the friends that they might have chosen to interact with might not have been available, leaving them with friend options that were less interesting to them. This may have been a bright new opportunity or an unfortunate poor choice.

Regardless of the friend group, the inability to interact as they had been likely took a toll on every child, with some faring worse than others. Returning to school may not solve this issue as depression tends to become its own issue that is difficult to overcome. Think of depression as a deep well. Just one misstep and a person can fall into the well, but it takes the right tools, effort, and several steps to climb out of it.

If your child/adolescent is having a particularly difficult time pulling out of depression or even a general funk, we suggest seeking professional help. Schools may have a counselor on staff or may be offering group opportunities focusing on returning to school. Outside counseling is an additional option, as is medication.

Here are some key points to consider if your child or adolescent is seemingly depressed or reports depressed mood:

- Depressed mood is the most frequent indicator of possible depression, but irritability can also be the main symptom.

- Normalize the "normal" feelings of the pandemic that are present at this time (e.g., moodiness, frustration, loneliness) but do not dismiss your child's feelings if they report that what they are experiencing is more serious than typical.

- Excessive thoughts about death, dying, and suicide are generally *not* part of normal feelings related to the pandemic.

- Feelings of loss, grief, and uncertainty of the future can be normal feelings during the pandemic.

- Be aware that your child may be gathering information about depression online, which can both help and harm the situation. Professional assessment and help trumps the internet diagnosis.

- Assuming your child was not depressed prior to the pandemic, help your child recognize the situational nature of their depression rather than accepting it as part of their identity.

- Scheduling positive activities and staying active are good initial interventions.

- Exercise, healthy eating, and time spent outside can be very helpful for depression. In addition, engaging in activities such as homework or other meaningful tasks is useful. However, kids (and even adults) often find it difficult to engage in these activities when they are depressed. Have honest discussions with your child to find activities that are more fun or at least less onerous.

- Scheduling time with friends, going to get a fun coffee, feeding the birds at the park, playing the guitar outside, playing a game with family, and the like may be fun, positive activities for the child.

- Remember that depression tends to make nothing sound fun. You are encouraging them to engage in activities that previously were fun or that have the potential to be fun.
- Social isolation is clearly linked to depression. Find ways to re-engage in social activities.
- Talk about the losses and fears that your child/adolescent has about the current situation as well as the future. Discuss together how you envision your child surviving this time. Help your child see the courage within themselves to move forward.

OTHER CONCERNS FOR RETURN TO SCHOOL

> *"Difficult roads often lead to beautiful destinations. The best is yet to come"*.

—— ZIG ZIGLER

> *"When we fail to set boundaries and hold people accountable, we feel used and mistreated"*.

—BRENE 'BROWN

CHAPTER 20

Sleep Schedule

Regardless of their age, many children and adolescents have drifted from their normal school-year sleep schedule. Both children and parents may have difficulty adjusting to the school's start and finish times. Some families choose to adopt a "get prepared"stance wherein they prepare for the sleep change by going to bed earlier and earlier in the week or weeks leading up to school return. Other families choose a "jump in" approach wherein they let the cards fall where they may and let nature take care of the change. After the first day or two of school, the child will be tired and will naturally go to bed earlier.

As you can imagine, there are many permutations in between these two strategies. We encourage you to consider not only which is best for the parents, but also which is most acceptable to the kids. It is easiest to create behavior change when all parties agree to the strategy and rationale of the plan, especially for teens.

Regardless of the plan that your family chooses to adopt, the following suggestions may prove beneficial:

- Try to allow the child/adolescent to wake on their own with an alarm. Parents can provide a check-in or provide back up as needed.
- Unfortunately, sometimes parents are more motivated for the child to get up and ready for school than the child is. Parents may need to get themselves to work and are on a timeline or they may simply want to get this portion of the day completed. Parents may believe that it would be a poor reflection on them if they are not able to get their child to school on time (which is usually more of an issue in early education years).
- Parents may want to help their child whom they believe is simply not capable of waking themselves. The tardies that would accrue may stand in the way of their child's grades or extracurricular participation, and the parent doesn't want their child to suffer unnecessarily due to inability to wake.
- If your child has such difficulty waking that mornings are a battlefield and sometimes the child wins and doesn't even

attend school that day or arrives substantially late, then you are likely dealing with an oppositional child. Oppositionality is addressed elsewhere and is its own larger issue. However, if this is a new skill, you are in great shape to help them become successful.

- Consider a musical alarm - waking to happy music may help your child start the day joyously.

- Some people like a blaring alarm that jars them from sleep, whereas others prefer a gentle tone that increases in volume if they do not wake. Perhaps your child could experiment with both so as to determine their preference.

- Begin by setting the alarm at the actual desired wake time; don't begin by allowing for multiple snoozes! Make adjustments only if you must. Two snooze-button hits equates to eighteen minutes of broken, poor sleep that could have been restful.

- In general, it's easier to alter a sleep schedule by maintaining a specific wake time than by trying to alter bedtime. In other words, bed time might have some variation, but wake time should be fairly consistent.

- You can set a time for being in bed (or being in their room), but it is very difficult to dictate sleep. In general, screens before bed can have a negative impact on sleep, but this can be somewhat offset by use of orange tones; the iPhone has a specific setting that changes the color tone of the screen at times that you choose. You could run a family experiment to determine if reducing screens before bed results in better sleep and/or easier waking.

- Good bedtime activities include reading, looking at picture books, small games (sudoku, word search, crosswords), meditation, prayer and/or gratitude practice, mindfulness exercises, and any other quiet activity that can allow for drowsiness. Every person is different, so each list of "go to" ideas will be different.

- Stressing about lack of sleep can sometimes be worse than the lack of sleep itself! Whether it is parental worry or child/adolescent worry, it is good to remember that many sleep issues will resolve themselves and that many people go through sleep disturbances at some point in their lives.

CHAPTER 21

Early Morning Drowsiness and Slowness to Get Ready

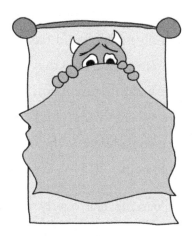

S ome people seem to drag in the morning more than others, and that includes children of all ages. Sometimes dragging is part of oppositional behavior, which is addressed in Chapter 12 and is its own issue. Many children are drowsy in the morning, and it is not oppositional but rather situational. For those children who have not returned to in-person classes, morning may have become quite relaxed, allowing for drowsy mornings.

Even kids who are usually quite good at getting up and on their way may have some difficulty returning to the typical school-day routine. Unfortunately, getting ready may have been a family battleground long before COVID. Often, morning difficulties can be viewed as a poor match between the parent's style and the child's style. When the styles match fairly well, the morning tends to pass much more smoothly than when the styles conflict.

Sometimes parents underestimate their child's capability and overcompensate by becoming more rigid and putting the responsibility on themselves. The child hasn't been required to be responsible for their time and so they don't practice being independent. An honest family discussion during which as many morning activities are given to the child (as is developmentally appropriate) should be considered. If the child has difficulty, then the parent is available to help.

Unfortunately, many parents feel overly responsible for making certain that their child isn't late, has their hair brushed, etc. and don't trust their child to do everything correctly. Sometimes, this is indeed true. But often the child simply hasn't practiced these skills because a parent was doing them. It may be time to allow the child to make some mistakes as they learn how to be responsible for their own morning routine.

If your child is dragging while making the adjustment to school wake times, the following suggestions may be helpful in creating a more pleasant morning:

- For younger children, consider bright music and lights in the morning. It should be music that your child enjoys; keep the focus on your child.

- Breakfasts should be convenient and hopefully not create arguments. For some families this may mean a fully cooked breakfast meal and for others it may mean a grab-n-go style of eating. Perhaps you want to decide the night before or have a set schedule (Monday is oatmeal). Adolescents may not want to eat at all, may eat at school, or may need much fuel to get started on their day. Many kids eat the same thing every day. For most parents, it is not the battle that they have to win. Making it pleasant while meeting the child's needs is fantastic.

- Some kids linger at the breakfast table and can't focus after eating. You may need to adjust your schedule of morning activities accordingly.

- Each step of the way when planning the morning, talk with your child and try to accommodate their wishes as much as possible, without being burdensome on yourself. The parents are the rulers of the household, but they can be benevolent rulers and consider the wishes of their people.

- If your child has difficulty getting everything completed in the morning, consider a checklist of morning activities. In addition, some kids may benefit from trying to keep the same order of activities in the routine. Use caution to not add more activities, such as "check off your activities when done." unless absolutely necessary. The list could also simply be a "before you head out the door" checklist to make certain things were done.

- Habit is a powerful tool. Even if significant effort is required to establish a good morning routine, dividends will likely pay out in the end. The best time to develop good morning habits is when children are young, but take heart, it's not too late.

- Set up as much the night before as is possible. Perhaps keep shoes by the door, put their backpack in order, locate jackets as needed, prep lunch as much as possible.

- Prepare for mistakes. If your child is continually forgetting to brush their hair, put an extra brush in the car. If they need medicine before school but tend to forget or run late, have a water bottle in the car specifically for medicine. It's ok if the preparation for mistakes becomes the go-to strategy, because it works well!

CHAPTER 22

Withdrawal from Social Media and Other Social Technology

F or thousands of reasons, children, adolescents, and even adults have become heavily reliant on social media and social technology, such as video games, streaming activities, and news scrolling. With the return to in-person education, time spent doing many of these activities will naturally decrease, as there simply isn't time. But they will serve as powerful distractors and may compete with after-school activities.

We want to be clear that we do not believe that social media and social technology, in and of themselves, are uniformly detrimental. In fact, it seems clear that they will be in our future and each one of us must learn how to manage our time and the emotional energy spent on these activities. No doubt many parents feel like parents of the 1930s who wished that TV was a fad and thought that if we just ignored it, it might just go away.

But like most technological advances, this one is likely to evolve, but not go away. Kids will live in a world in which they must learn to monitor themselves and find the balance that fits their needs, knowing that this balance is ever changing. The goal is for children and adolescents to learn this skill rather than simply have limits dictated to them.

If the child or adolescent doesn't understand the value of the restrictions, when the imposed limits are lifted the child/adolescent will not have learned anything about how to regulate their use. They are also unlikely to be *motivated* to regulate themself. In addition, the limits placed by authority figures can result in rebellion, scheming, and unnecessary defiance. This DOES NOT mean that limits shouldn't be set. When possible, however, kids should be part of the discussion regarding the limits and understand the parental views that explain their value. Keep the following in mind:

- Pick and choose your parental fights. To help your child understand why you think their social media time should be limited, you need to understand your own rationale beyond "a good parent would do this." Your child and your family are unique.

- You can always run experiments. If your child maintains that they can be on their screen until bedtime without problems in the morning, you can run the experiment, gather data, and then reconvene to examine the data and revise the plan.

- Try to be understanding about the withdrawal process, which includes their desire for low-level rest activity, as well as the potential social fallout from not "snapping back when on a streak" (on Snapchat).

- Consider setting a designated time period or time allotment for social media as an experiment. After a period of time, gather to determine how it is working and make changes as needed.

- Think creatively to increase activities that automatically decrease time spent on social media or with social technology.

- Some of our return to social media and/or technology is a habit. Like most habits, it can be difficult to change and is unlikely to be like just flipping a switch. Be patient but consistent.

- Allow your child to help in planning for reduction of time spent on social media or technology.

- Several smartphones have timers that will give a warning when the set time limit is approaching. You can choose which apps and the length of time that you would like to set limits for.

- Third-party apps also allow for limiting time or exposure to certain apps. When using these, remember that the end goal is for the child/adolescent to limit themselves. Like adults, they may choose to use external help, such as apps, to achieve their goals.

- Another tool to limit social media time would be to use grayscale. Photos not in color are less exciting to spend an hour reviewing.

- Again, the goal is for the child/adolescent to limit themselves. When appropriate, parents can help identify apps or other aids to serve as reminders or alternatives to limit social media or technology.

- A possible experiment, particularly with adolescents: Take a week-long hiatus from social media. Think of it as a "juice cleanse" for the mind. This strategy can be very effective when the adolescent acknowledges that they are on their phone too much. Let them know, in this case, that it is elective, not a punishment. It is an experiment in better understanding the impact of social media on themselves.

- The documentary *Social Dilemma* may offer an opportunity for good discussions with your teen. Again, the best conversations occur when your teen has agreed to have the discussion.

CHAPTER 23

After-School Homework

For elementary school: In general, research suggests that for typically developing elementary school children in schools with approved curricula, homework does not necessarily add benefit to their education. It is usually better for children to be developing leisure interests, enjoying unstructured time, and building initiative. Appropriately limit excessive time spent in homework for school-age children. If your elementary school-aged child is spending an excessive amount of time on homework, it is time to discuss options with their teachers.

Many teachers assign homework with an idea of how much time it should take to complete. Usually the time needed is thirty minutes or less for most activities. If your child is requiring longer or the activities are adding up to much longer, consider reviewing the situation with the teacher and making appropriate decisions for your child. While you want your child to complete homework, you also have the larger picture of your child developing an appreciation or love of learning and enjoying childhood.

For middle and high school: Be aware of the amount of time spent "feeling" like they are doing homework, when reality might indicate that screens or other activities are prolonging this time. Encourage, as much as possible, working in a sanctioned spot (either the main part of the house or in their own room depending upon their age and maturity.). Teach good study habits and efficient completion of homework.

Discuss how you, the parent, studied effectively (or didn't!) and allow them to experiment with a variety of methods to determine the style that fits their needs. Encourage them to discuss alternative study methods with their teachers or tutors as well. Consider allowing kids to invite friends to study together. Change the venue for homework. Especially as kids emerge from COVID, they may really love the idea of working in a library or coffee shop! Help your child recognize that they are developing their personal style of studying and that rarely is the best method in college the same one used in sixth grade.

Remember that they may have reduced stamina for attending all-day classes and then doing additional homework at night. It may take time to find their rhythm. Approaching after-school work with an experimental attitude may help your child or adolescent find what works best for them. The best result may not be the same as their pre-COVID routine. Keep the following in mind:

- Plan a specific location for homework and have necessary items nearby.
- Snacks may be necessary items. Phones and other screens may not be - depends upon the student.
- Allow and encourage breaks as needed as the student builds their stamina, especially for homework that doesn't appeal to them.
- If your child is simultaneously beginning sport or exercise activities as they return to school, help them to recognize good habits rather than simply exhausting themselves (sleep, eating, time management, setting limits). Help your child to not overschedule and to recognize priorities.
- For elementary school children, be wary of excessive homework that is occurring daily. Investigate to determine why it requires so much time and intervene to find a better balance.
- Allow your older adolescent to study with friends if that increases motivation and productivity.

- Allow your adolescent to study in different settings (e.g., library, coffee shop, park) if that increases motivation and productivity.
- Encourage your child to ask about the study habits of others to better understand study options. The student can then experiment with different methods for different classes to determine the best fit for them.
- Be understanding about the fatigue induced by all-day in-person classes that are followed by homework. Help your child build their stamina and feel success along the way.

CHAPTER 24
Rebuilding Stamina

When a person has an injury that requires rest and sedentary activities, deconditioning is likely to occur. We potentially decline in muscle strength, cardiovascular health, cognitive stamina, as well as emotional stamina. Analogously, COVID-related restrictions may have led to a bit of deconditioning; mentally, physically, and emotionally.

As children and teens return to the normal stresses of day-to-day functioning, we may find that some seem a bit fragile. That's what happens when we aren't faced with the experiences that lead us to feel calm and competent.

If you see this occur in your family, a good first step is not to panic, but rather to recognize the reduced stamina for what it is: a somewhat predictable, temporary phase.

Next, don't automatically assume that this is evidence that you need to rescue your child or reduce the stressors. In fact, the best approach may be to normalize the typical stressors of life and help your child recognize that they can cope. Discuss ways to handle stress.

For instance, it may be useful to remind a child that low blood sugar may reduce self-control and thereby things may seem worse than they actually are. Encourage them to label the situation, step back and solve problems, brainstorm, and make plans to address those components of the situation over which they have control.

Talk with kids about the idea that not all stress is "bad." In fact, the word "eustress" refers to "good" stress. Help kids recognize that the flip side of stress can be boredom. And boredom is no picnic either! In fact, it's stressful.

The stress of extra work, additional social pressures, time pressures, lack of downtime, and lack of free time is also an indicator of learning, growing, having fun things to do with friends, and staying busy. Recognize the importance of perception while rebuilding stamina.

While encouraging your child or adolescent to recondition their stamina to meet the needs of in-person school and life, be generous with empathy. It is a fine line between understanding their, and possibly your own, exhaustion and allowing for too much avoidance of effort.

Finally, as parents, be aware of the natural desire to prevent children from any form of suffering. Allow them to experience the stress and later, when it has passed, point out that exact fact. Review how they were able to survive (and thrive) even when they thought they couldn't.

CHAPTER 25

Educational Losses

As we emerge from school closures and online learning, there are likely to be lost educational milestones for many children. Each school district will inevitably have specific and different plans on how to address these holes in the knowledge of their students. Logically, it seems that we can expect a period of assessment to gather information about where these missing pieces may be. While schools will certainly be making plans to address this, many families may wish to be proactive and begin addressing any educational deficits immediately.

It might be best for parents to focus on fundamentals of what is expected at various levels of education. Consider seeking private tutors, learning centers, and even state guidelines on educational expectations for children at various levels. The summer of 2021 may provide an excellent opportunity for catching up while day-to-day school demands are not present. It might be wise to pick just one or two areas to address. Don't expect your child to catch up on an entire year of work over the summer months. Keep it basic and manageable.

Parents should keep in mind that if they find that their child is behind educationally, they are likely in good company. Many children will have gaps in their expected academic achievement. This fact is likely to result in system-wide solutions that will be implemented at school. Keeping both parent and child anxiety in check will likely result in quicker gains in areas of deficit.

The majority of kids will be able to work a bit extra to return to their expected academic levels. Schools may find that those students who were lagging prior to the pandemic will be in greatest need of assistance and remediation.

If your child was struggling prior to the shutdown, we suggest that you consider obtaining assessment as early as possible, whether within or outside of the school system. Extra tutoring - which was previously considered something that could be helpful - may be an essential activity at this time. Keep the following in mind:

- Identify the grade-appropriate skills expected for your student to allow for assessment of strengths and weaknesses.

- Be aware of the school's procedures for assessment and intervention of academic progress.

- Don't feel pressured to overwhelm yourself or your child; go at a reasonable pace as you add remedial academic work to the schedule.

- If your child was having some academic difficulties prior to the shutdown, be aware that your student is likely to particularly benefit from some additional help and practice.

- Academic deficits may be related to age and grade levels of the student, with some at more risk than others. It is likely that many others of similar ages and grade levels will also be facing some difficulties as they quickly move to catch up.

- Academic deficits are likely to also be related to the type of instruction that they have been receiving during the pandemic. We would guess that completely online students are the most likely to suffer, but there will be great individual differences!

- If you have several children you will likely see variation in how certain academic subjects were affected by the shutdown. We suggest you focus on each individual child's needs rather than a broad based remediation plan. For example, some children will need help with math while others will have done well.

GENERAL CONCERNS FOR RETURN TO LIFE

> *"What man actually needs is not a tensionless state but rather the striving and struggling for some goal worthy of him. What he needs is not the discharge of tension at any cost, but the call of a potential meaning waiting to be fulfilled by him".*

———VIKTOR FRANKL

> *"Argue as if you re right, but listen as if you re wrong (and be willing to change your mind.) Make the most respectful interpretation of the other person s perspective".*

———GREG LUKIANOFF / JONATHAN HAIDT

CHAPTER 26

Fostering Resilience

In recent years, many authors have expounded upon the necessity of developing resilience, grit, anti-fragility, and other characteristics in our children. The idea behind each of these has been that children have increasingly become stalled in their emotional and intellectual growth by seemingly small hurdles. These hurdles, common in childhood, have not typically been associated with paralyzing or upsetting emotions.

Each of these words (grit, resilience, etc.) chosen by various authors seems to focus on our need to enhance self-efficacy, belief in one's ability to overcome obstacles, and to foster forward movement.

Students who report that some learning content is too disturbing to learn or even discuss seem to be an indicator of this decreased resiliency.

Certainly there are several topics of learning that are distressing; history is filled with many examples. But the learning, understanding, and discussion of these events and beliefs, at age-appropriate levels, are important as children become young adults and young citizens.

These discussions may lead to challenges of belief systems. Empathetic understanding is likely to be enhanced as kids hear reasonable perspectives that differ from their own. When we encounter challenges to our beliefs, we often learn to hone our arguments and build critical-thinking skills. We learn that we are competent, capable, and even strong. We are often stronger in the long run.

It makes sense that, as parents, one goal is to allow these challenges for our children while providing scaffolding as needed and a safe landing in case of falls. Unfortunately, parents today are often given a very different message. They are encouraged to preempt suffering. Parents are told to quickly swing into action to prevent/address perceived bullying, failures, and other hardships. The notion that childhood should be smooth, blissful, and pleasant predominates.

This seems to dovetail with another message being sent to parents today: Your adolescent cannot make mistakes; if they do, they will have no future. The idea that any academic or behavioral mishaps will have grave repercussions upon their future (no college, no job, no family, no life) is perpetuated by parents, peers, teachers, and the general public. In our offices, we often see kids who are heavily burdened by the gravity of each move, during a time when they should be allowed to experiment and make mistakes.

It seems natural that parents would like to prevent any such devastating mistakes from being made. This attempt to prevent suffering might be thought of as "paving the road for the child." But the cost is high, limiting the adolescent's ability to make their own decisions and mistakes. The most efficient learning comes from doing. By doing, we make mistakes, course correct, fall down, and pick ourselves back up.

The experience of realizing that problems can be faced and managed is incredibly empowering. If we constantly pave the way for children, we rob them of the opportunity to realize that they are tougher and more capable than they realized and that they can cope with distress.

The reality of childhood is that it is often hard. And the struggle is what leads to competent, well-functioning adults. Think of all the hard stuff that kids have to endure, even in the best of times: not being the best at things, losing games, struggling to learn, feeling left out, not getting to do what they want, disappointing parents, losing grandparents, divorce of parents, the list goes on. But learning to successfully manage the bumps and bruises of childhood ultimately leads to a sense of competence and the ability to cope with life's inevitable trials.

COVID-19 has certainly presented children and families with challenging situations and hardships: death of loved ones, isolation from friends and extended family, interruptions to education, and postponed activities (sports, vacations, birthdays). However, there are opportunities in these difficulties to help children build a sense of competence and coping.

Discussing how COVID has affected your family and particularly your child is a good beginning. Allow your child to review what has been successful and less successful in their attempts to cope with changes over the past year.

We also suggest discussing how things will be different in the following year. Review how parents will be allowing them age-appropriate independence over their academics and their lifestyle. If you are choosing to oversee the child's efforts, discuss why you are doing this and review the plan to move toward independence.

The goal is to help your child achieve and desire more independence. Understandably, as parents, you will be watching for your child to make good decisions, while knowing that some poor decisions will necessarily be made! Not too many (if any) adults have made their way without mistakes. Keep the following points in mind:

- Avoid paving the road for your child.

- Do not shield children from the reality of death. Teach them about expected reactions to death, model coping, provide them with actionable rituals to celebrate lives, and enrich their understanding of your religious teachings about life/death. Teach them to cope and suggest to them that it is possible to be strong, respectful, and reliable at a funeral.

- It is perfectly reasonable to limit exposure to excessive news, especially for younger children. But provide children with age-appropriate information about events in the world around them.

- Converse with kids about how they have become stronger during the pandemic. Help them to see themselves as brave and, if appropriate, even heroic.

- Help your child reframe mistakes by learning from them, identify how to avoid the same mistake if possible, and discuss consequences if necessary.

- When age-appropriate, share mistakes you or your friends and family have made and how they have learned. This offers both validation for being typical as well as vicarious learning about dealing with difficult challenges. Boost their confidence to make good decisions themselves.

- Help your child tolerate challenging information or situations by emphasizing the importance of these challenges and offering ways to cope or manage their discomfort.

- For some children, certain education topics or discussion topics cause a great deal of emotional pain. It is easiest to escape by avoiding: my child shouldn't have to complete this assignment. Efforts should be made to decrease avoidance behavior and learn how to cope with difficult topics.

CHAPTER 27

Keep What is Good

The negatives of our experiences with COVID-19 seem obvious, but we shouldn't overlook the positives that we have learned or gained. In fact, we should be particularly mindful of holding onto the benefits and maintaining them in our lives moving forward. Most of the positives have been born out of the reality that we've had nowhere to go and thus nothing to do. We've been forced to generate new ways to entertain ourselves.

Many families have found that their lifestyles have long been overbooked. Trying to juggle school, soccer, gymnastics, musical instrument, church activities, tutoring and test prep, and family commitments has taken a toll. This is even more pronounced in families with more than one child! The shutdown has helped many families to recalibrate their desired activities. This appreciation for the limits and boundaries of our time should be maintained. It is truly one of the silver linings of this experience.

The appreciation of family time is another silver lining. This refers to both the enjoyment of time together as well as the importance of time apart. We need both our time together and our time alone! Children, adolescents, and parents need time alone, and often that includes privacy. This is a great thing to keep from our shutdown experience. Everyone needs some time to themselves. When children return home from in-person school, remember that they have been surrounded by people all day and may desire some time alone. Schedule family time, such as dinner or before bed, but enjoy time alone as well.

In addition to lifestyle and family changes, many individuals have gained a renewed awareness of the importance of community. Appreciation for grocery store workers, hospital workers, teachers, restaurant workers, and delivery workers has never been higher. Many families have relied on these individuals 'continuing in their professions to allow others to have their essential needs met. The workers in these fields are often underappreciated, and during the shutdown they became vital. Community awareness of their service has been a huge positive. Hopefully we will continue to appreciate their efforts.

Some potential positive experiences include the following:

Special time with family:

- Family game nights
- Family meals
- Sharing our entertainment (family movies, family TV shows, family video game play and tournaments)
- Sharing skills: kids helping parents with technology.
- Gain appreciation for alone time for children
- Over-scheduled isn't always good; it has been nice to have relaxed days and relaxed evenings
- Cooking and baking more often or as a family

Time for ourselves:

- Pleasure in relaxing; because you can't go anywhere, you stay in jammies and snuggle
- Reading for pleasure or education
- Time to reflect on important values and prioritize our lives
- Time to create (such as crafts, writing, videos)

Time outdoors:

- Picnics
- Outdoor exercise or even just walking around the neighborhood
- Enjoying your backyard (or front yard)

- Enjoying local outdoor areas such as lakes, parks, hiking trails

Friends and Society:

- Gathering in large six-foot distanced circles to laugh and share. Going forward, we won't need the distancing, but the gathering and sharing we should keep.
- Ordering take-out and delivery from a variety of local restaurants
- Tipping well; being grateful for the jobs that others do for us.
- Learning the lesson of what you can and what you can't control
- We have survived a very difficult time, all of us #alonetogether
- Life is often hard, and we survived a hard time, people joined together, thought innovatively, and worked together.
- People may have very different opinions, but our desired outcomes are often similar: physical and emotional safety, meaningful employment, enjoyment of friends and family, tolerance from others for our own beliefs.
- One day at a time, we have persevered, and we will continue forward.

Add Your Own:

- _____

Keep What is Good

- _____
- _____
- _____
- _____
- _____

CHAPTER 28

Empathy and Tolerance of Others 'Beliefs

The pandemic struck during an interesting historical period. Social media and other factors contributed to a highly polarized America prior to its arrival. People have strong opinions, and they have platforms on which to state those opinions. Twitter, Facebook, TikTok, Instagram, and various other social media platforms have allowed millions of Americans to voice their satisfaction and dissatisfaction with all aspects of American culture.

The fact that social media has the powerful ability to aggregate the voices of Americans has both pros and cons. The pros include entertainment, sense of belonging, and expression of our individuality. Perhaps the greatest con lies within how social media platforms prioritize content shown to each individual.

Several social media platforms use algorithms to match the information a person sees with the information that a person believes. If you love reading about too much rain in Nevada, you will be shown more stories about too much rain in Nevada. This feeds our strong propensity toward confirmation bias: the tendency to seek information that confirms our pre-existing beliefs. It serves to further solidify the belief that you already held.

Confirmation bias works against critical thinking because it specifically denies the person the opportunity to examine alternative theories and beliefs. (Perhaps there is *not* too much rain in Nevada.) How can we fully examine an issue if we do not examine it from all sides? To overcome confirmation bias we must encounter opposing and/or challenging views. It is one of the great gifts of America's freedom of speech. These algorithms reduce our exposure to alternative views and lead us to become further entrenched in our current positions and views. It's like having millions of "yes men" surrounding us at all times.

Particularly during the beginning months of our awareness of COVID, we suffered from a lack of reliable information. This is a new virus! Although it was known to be deadly, we did not have good evidence regarding exactly how deadly. With little to no information on how it transmits, how easily it transmits, how lethal it is, and what factors make people vulnerable. We were left to assume the worst. In addition to not having the data to help us proceed, we were offered various opinions by medical professionals and politicians who often disagreed, even among themselves! And, frankly, some sought to mislead us.

This void of reliable information left people holding widely differing opinions on how best to respond to the COVID pandemic. Some people have voiced very strong beliefs and have been angry and outraged when others disagreed. Anger flares from belief that people are willingly and knowingly choosing to "kill grandma" and we have lost our personal freedoms.

The year 2020 saw great moments of people working together, but it has also seen continued polarization and lack of empathy toward others. As restrictions lift, and particularly as children return to school, we encourage empathy and tolerance for others 'beliefs. As adults, we make our choices and are willing to accept the consequences of those choices. Children, however, are returning to an environment of diverse opinions and family responses to the threat of COVID.

How we view the different ways in which families responded to the pandemic is reminiscent of the way we view the differences in driving speeds - the person driving faster than you is crazy, the person driving slower than you is a fool, and the person driving the same speed as you is just annoying.

Regardless of their responses, other people are often viewed as either being too cautious, not cautious enough, or just right - but we're watching for them to slip! We can easily become annoyed by the decisions made by other families and almost no two families will respond in exactly the same way.

We encourage you to discuss with your child the different responses to COVID and why others might choose a different path than the one chosen by your family. We strongly encourage helping children avoid illness shaming, wherein they believe that anyone who contracts COVID is obviously bad because it indicates that they were being too risky. We also encourage the avoidance of shaming those who continue to wear masks and are having difficulty returning to a pre-COVID lifestyle. People should not be shamed for being cautious at a different level than others.

This discussion is a great opportunity to examine the importance of empathy and tolerance of the beliefs of others. Perhaps our goal as a society will include both unification where possible and tolerance where differences exist.

Example: Recently, a conscientious adolescent girl admitted in an initial therapy session that she was worried that she would unknowingly bring COVID into the therapist office, endangering the middle-aged (ish) therapist. Her concern was addressed by pointing out that COVID is not a character flaw, it's a virus. And that's what viruses do, they spread. Furthermore, it was pointed out that by agreeing to be in the same room together (with masks and distancing), something of an unwritten contract had been formed. It essentially read: neither of us will knowingly attend sessions ill or after clear exposure. Otherwise, we meet without blame. We are taking what we feel to be reasonable risks.

CHAPTER 29

All Living is Risky

During the pandemic, people have become frightened of dying not only from COVID but also from general complications (hospitalization, ventilators), as well as of contracting it and suffering a terrible illness that can last for weeks and may result in long-term symptoms. Experiencing this level of fear has raised our collective anxiety and fear levels as well. Cautious people have had a tendency to become even more cautious.

If you have been surrounded by family, friends, and co-workers who are also cautious, this fear tends to grow for the group as a whole. This phenomenon is present for both fear and anger. Humans are vulnerable to confirmation bias, which is our tendency to locate information that confirms or validates our beliefs. Confirmation bias, along with many other human biases, tends to exacerbate our emotions. We get pumped up with fear or anger when we have experience-confirming information or opinions.

Some families will be particularly vulnerable to anxiety concerning the return to in-person school. Perhaps their communities, friends, family members, and respected professionals have supported their caution, and likely for understandable reasons. But when the time comes to allow for safe return to school, some of these families will continue to have difficulties. Even normal, typical, pre-COVID risks will feel too risky.

It is certainly understandable that some individuals, following an entire year (and more!) of being concerned and cautious, will have difficulty relaxing back into their previous lifestyle. After running a marathon, you don't finish and then pop right back into regular breathing. You experience a recovery period that is directly related to the intensity of the workout. In fact, often our bodies are still recovering long after we perceive that we are back to normal.

The same is true for anxiety and fear. Following a traumatic event, often our fear is increased for a period of time; we don't simply return to everyday as usual immediately. We talk about being shaken, on edge, still adjusting, and other terms to indicate that what we are experiencing is a normal part of trauma recovery.

In Chapter 5 we discussed how to cope with fear. Specifically, we discussed a difference between realistic and unrealistic threats/fears. COVID concerns are particularly complex in that some of our collective fear is realistic, while some is unrealistic. Even our understanding of which fears are realistic has changed as more information about the virus and its transmission has come to the fore.

Here we are addressing fears that are not necessarily unrealistic but perhaps are excessive. The statement, "I might catch a disease." is realistic. The devastation associated with the thought, "I might catch a disease" could be an under-response or an over-response (excessive).

For example, "A tornado might hit our house" is simply a statement. (It is more likely to be true in some parts of America than in others!) If a person refuses to leave the bedroom of their house and is constantly checking weather reports and looking at the sky for ominous signs, then we can see that their stated fear is excessive.

When fears are either excessive or unrealistic, the greatest improvements are associated with exposure therapy. We must accept that a certain amount of risk exists. No amount of protection is guaranteed at 100 percent. In the preceding example, the person is encouraged to leave the bedroom and eventually leave the house. They are also encouraged to decrease checking both weather reports and the sky (to the extent possible). The person should go toward the risk and try to engage in living.

Accepting that risk exists is an important step within the exposure. Life is inherently risky. Luckily, most of us are able to tune out the risks that surround us daily. We have rational information about "what is the likelihood that ___ will happen," and we comfort ourselves. We watch others and follow their example: *They don t seem bothered, so I shouldn t be bothered.* We have a sense of self-efficacy. *Even if this happens, I ll be able to survive.*

Some people have difficulty accepting risk, and often things may feel riskier than they actually are. The point, however, is worth repeating: Life is risky! It has always had risks and always will. We try to minimize predictable risks. But even if we try to eliminate every possible risk, trouble will still find us. Life is unpredictable in both joyous and tragic ways. Often, we simply don't have enough information to even assess our true risk. What is the alternative: not accepting the risks, simply don't live, don't go anywhere, don't do anything?

People can sustain the "not living" approach and can even convince themselves that it's not so bad. We can have food brought in, entertainment is readily downloaded, human interaction can be virtual . . . but is this really living? It may be surviving, but it is certainly not thriving. At the point when our survival is impairing our lives rather than enhancing or actually protecting them, changes should be made.

There is no method by which we are guaranteed safety.

A tragic example of life's unpredictability and the impossibility of preventing all danger comes to mind.

Years ago, there was a news story about a man in Florida who had fallen asleep, snug in his bed, family members in the next room, when a sinkhole opened underneath his bed. The bed with the man on it was consumed by the sinkhole. He was never found. A sinkhole! Who predicts that? Should every person have a ground survey conducted to determine if the ground underneath their bedroom could possibly become a sinkhole? (Please do not do this!)

The moral of the story is that you just never know. You can be doing something that seems perfectly safe - no risk - and the worst can happen! COVID is similar. As we emerge from the pandemic, we enter the same unpredictable world that we left a year ago in an attempt to flatten the curve. We need to help children and teens develop the skills to face the world, with all its inherent risks. There really isn't an alternative. This is not new. This has always been life.

ADDITIONAL READING

Brown, Brene'. *Rising Strong: The Reckoning, The Rumble, The Revolution.* (New York: Spiegel & Grau, 2015).

Brown, Brene'. *The Gifts of Imperfection: Let Go of Who You Think You re Supposed to Be and Embrace Who You Are.* (Center City, MN: Hazelden, 2010).

Graham, Linda. *Bouncing Back.* (California: New World Library, 2013).

Haidt, Johathan. *The Righteous Mind: Why Good People Are Divided by Politics and Religion.* (New York: Random House, 2012).

Hoefle, Vicki. *Duct Tape Parenting: A Less Is More Approach to Raising Respectful, Responsible, and Resilient Kids.* (Brookline, MA: Bibliomotion, 2012).

Korb, Alex. *The Upward Spiral: Using Neuroscience to Reverse the Course of Depression, One Small Change at a Time.* (Oakland, CA: New Harbinger, 2015).

Lahey, Jessica. *The Gift of Failure: How the Best Parents Learn to Let Go So Their Children Can Succeed.* (New York: Harper, 2015).

Lukanoff, Greg, and Haidt, Jonathan. *The Coddling of the American Mind: How Good Intentions and Bad Ideas Are Setting Up a Generation for Failure.* (New York: Penguin, 2018).

Melton, Glennon D. *Carry On, Warrior: The Power of Embracing Your Messy, Beautiful Life.* (New York: Scribner, 2013).

Mogel, Wendy. *The Blessing of a B-: Raising Resilient Teenagers.* (New York: Scribner, 2010)

Mogel, Wendy. *The Blessing of a Skinned Knee: Raising Self-Reliant Children.* (New York: Scribner, 2001).

Peterson, Jordan B. *12 Rules for Life: An Antidote to Chaos.* (Toronto: Penguin, 2018).

Shaywitz, Sally, and Shaywitz, Jonathan. *Overcoming Dyslexia: Second Edition, Completely Revised and Updated.* (New York: Alfred A. Knopf, 2020).

AUTHORS

BETH LUSBY, Ph.D.. has been licensed as a psychologist in Texas since 1998. In 2004, she opened Cornerstone Assessment and Guidance Center, LLC in Colleyville, Texas. Her practice provides clinical and neuropsychological services to children, adolescents, and families. Dr. Lusby graduated from the University of Colorado magna cum laude with a B.A. in psychology.

She attended the University of Louisville, in Kentucky, where she received both an M.A. and a Ph.D. in clinical psychology. After completing an APA approved pre-doctoral internship at the

University of Texas Health Sciences Center, Houston, Dr. Lusby completed her postdoctoral work with a neuropsychology practice in Dallas (Pate Rehabilitation). Dr. Lusby is a member of the National Academy of Neuropsychology and the Texas Psychological Association.

SHERYL R. JACKSON, Ph.D. received her degree in clinical psychology in 1994 from Louisiana State University. She specializes in the assessment and treatment of anxiety disorders and OCD. She was an associate professor at the University of Alabama at Birmingham Department of Psychiatry and Behavioral Neurobiology for thirteen years where she ran the Anxiety and OCD Program.

While there, she was the Internship Training Director as well as Assistant Resident Training Director. She taught in the UAB Department of Psychology as adjunct faculty. For the past thirteen years Dr. Jackson has been in private practice specializing in anxiety disorders and OCD. She has travelled with Cross Country Education offering continuing education to mental health practitioners.

Dr. Jackson has three young-adult children. Each of her children has been in either high school or college during this pandemic experience. Personally and professionally, Dr. Jackson has been keenly aware the effects of the pandemic upon children, adolescents, and families.

Made in the USA
Monee, IL
21 September 2021